Moving Averages
Simplified

By Clif Droke

MARKETPLACE BOOKS
Columbia, MD

MARKETPLACE BOOKS

Simplified Series

Technical Analysis Simplified *by Clif Droke*

Elliott Wave Simplified *by Clif Droke*

Moving Averages Simplified *by Clif Droke*

Other ground-breaking books in the Marketplace Books Series:

The Precision Profit Float Indicator: Powerful Techniques to Exploit Price and Volume *by Steve Woods*

Trader's Guide to Technical Analysis *by C. Colburn Hardy*

Commodity Options: Spectacular Options With Limited Risk *by Larry Spears*

Trend Forecasting: Unleashing the Hidden Power of Intermarket Analysis to Beat the Market *by Louis B. Mendelsohn*

7 Chart Patterns That Consistently Make Money *by Ed Downs*

Trading, Sex, and Dying: The Heart of a Gambler *by Juel E. Anderson*

The ARMS Index *by Richard Arms, Jr.*

The New Market Wizards: Conversations With America's Top Traders *by Jack D. Schwager*

McMillan On Options *by Lawrence G. McMillan*

The Art of Short Selling *by Kathryn Staley*

Point and Figure Charting: Essential Applications for Forecasting and Tracking Market Prices *by Tom Dorsey*

The Trader's Tax Solution: Money Saving Strategies for the Serious Investor *by Ted Tesser*

"Nothing distills the essence of supply and demand like the chart. And nothing distills the chart quite like the moving average."

— Clif Droke

ISBN 1-883272-66-1

Printed in the United States of America

Contents

Introduction

Moving averages have long been used by investors and traders as an aid to analyzing price trends. Moving averages have the attribute of being able to smooth price fluctuations, making it easier to follow underlying trends with the naked eye. Used in conjunction with other technical indicators, or even with other averages, moving averages provide a reliable tool for beating the market a fair percentage of the time — once you know how to use them properly.

A growing number of traders are becoming aware of the tremendous profit potential that comes with integrating moving averages with a favored trading system. Books have already been written to teach the profitable application of moving averages in trading the markets, yet most fall short of this goal. One reason for this failing is that a basic working knowledge of moving averages is already common among countless thousands of traders. As any good trader knows, once a particular trading system becomes the common knowledge of the vast multitudes, it tends to lose its utility and reliability. Few

Used in conjunction with other technical indicators, or even with other averages, moving averages provide a reliable tool for beating the market a fair percentage of the time — once you know how to use them properly.

books on moving averages have gone beyond the plebeian in their attempts to explain how moving averages can be used to a trader's advantage.

Another problem with books that have addressed this subject is that they frequently err on the side of complexity. Experienced traders are aware that the more complex a given trading system is, the less often it provides useful trading signals. In the marketplace, as in most of life itself, simplicity is the essence of success. It is our philosophy, based on many years of study and real-time experience, that the more simple a trading method is, the more likely it will prove beneficial to the trader, and we have kept this principle in mind in producing this book.

> **It is our philosophy, based on many years of study and real-time experience, that the more simple a trading method is, the more likely it will prove beneficial to the trader, and we have kept this principle in mind in producing this book.**

One little known and widely overlooked aspect of moving averages is that they work best when used in conjunction with cycle analysis. The trader must have at least a basic understanding of market cycles in order to consistently use moving average analysis to his or her advantage. So crucial is cycle theory to the profitable employment of moving averages to any form of trading, that we felt compelled to include two chapters in this book dedicated to cycle analysis when used in conjunction with moving averages. Chapter 6, alone, should be worth the price of this book for the serious trader.

It is not within the scope of this book to focus exclusively on moving averages with reference to market cycles; nevertheless, a broad understanding of this application is necessary and should always be borne in mind when conducting moving average analysis. After all, moving averages are, essentially, smoothed out pricelines, which highlight the major trends and cycles that govern the underlying security. Aside from the cyclical element of moving average analysis, we also examine the more traditional forms of moving averages when used in conjunction with price, volume, and various technical indicators.

You will find throughout this work a number of "real-market" charts, supplied by BigCharts.com, which will greatly add to your understanding and comprehension of the principles this book aims to teach. Nothing but experience can ultimately assure consistent success in the markets, but the studies and examples included in this book will further your understanding of how moving averages, once properly implemented, will greatly enhance your trading success.

The studies and examples included in this book will further your understanding of how moving averages, once properly implemented, will greatly enhance your trading success.

CHAPTER 1

The Essence of Moving Averages:
What Every Successful Trader Should Know

The term "moving averages" is widely employed within the realm of financial analysis, and almost everyone has a basic comprehension of what they are and how they are used. Yet few truly understand the intricacies of moving averages and the many ways they can be used to maximize trading profits in the financial markets. A growing interest among the investing public about moving averages has spawned a number of books on the subject in recent years, yet few books, despite their merit, really come close to providing the essence of what moving averages are, and how and when they should be used. To that end, we have written this book with the hope that it will go far in aiding the serious trader or investor about the proper way of incorporating moving averages into his or her market analysis.

What is a moving average? A moving average is an indicator that shows the average value of a security's price over a period of time.[1] When calculating a moving average, a mathematical analysis of the security's average value over a predetermined time

A moving average is an indicator that shows the average value of a security's price over a period of time.

period is made. As the security's price changes, its average price moves up or down.

The five most commonly used types of moving averages are the simple, or arithmetic; the exponential; the triangular; the variable; and the weighted moving average. Moving averages can be calculated on any data series, including a security's open, high, low, close, volume, or other indicator. A moving average of another moving average is also commonly used in various forms of technical analysis.[2] This technique is used for purposes of tracking the price momentum of a stock or commodity and is constructed by averaging the moving average of the price being followed.

The only significant difference between the various types of moving averages is the weight assigned to the most recent price data. Simple moving averages apply equal weight to the prices. Exponential and weighted averages apply more weight to recent prices of the stock or commodity being followed. Triangular averages apply more weight to prices in the middle of the time period. And variable moving averages change the weighted based on the volatility of prices.[3]

Steven B. Achelis, in his book, *Technical Analysis From A to Z*, has written one of the most lucid explanations of moving averages that we have read, which we quote from at length:

"The most popular method of interpreting a moving average is to compare the relationship between a moving average of the security's price with the

When calculating a moving average, a mathematical analysis of the security's average value over a predetermined time period is made. As the security's price changes, its average price moves up or down. A buy signal is generated when the security's price rises above its moving average, and a sell signal is generated when the security's price falls below its moving average.

security's price itself. A buy signal is generated when the security's price rises above its moving average, and a sell signal is generated when the security's price falls below its moving average.

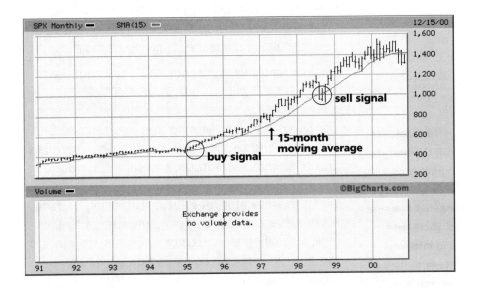

FIGURE 1-1: Simple Moving Average

This monthly S&P 500 bar chart illustrates a 15-month moving average. Note the buy and sell signals generated as the price moved above and below the moving average line.

Continues Achelis: "This type of moving average trading system is not intended to get you in at the exact bottom nor out at the exact top. Rather, it is designed to keep you in line with the security's price trend by buying shortly after the security's price bottoms and selling shortly after it tops.

"The critical element in a moving average is the number of time periods used in calculating the average. When using hindsight, you can always find a moving average that would have been profitable. . . . The key is to find a moving average that will be consistently profitable. The most popular moving average is the 39-week (or 200-day) moving average.

This moving average has an excellent track record in timing the major (long-term) market cycles.

"The length of a moving average should fit the market cycle you wish to follow. For example, if you determine that a security has a 40-day peak-to-peak cycle, the ideal moving average length would be 21 days calculated using the following formula:

$$\text{Ideal Moving Average Length} = \frac{\text{Cycle Length} + 1}{2}$$

In this book, we will concentrate primarily on price-only simple moving averages of short-term and intermediate-term time frames.

Continues Achelis: "Moving averages can also be calculated and plotted on indicators. The interpretation of an indicator's moving average is similar to the interpretation of a security's moving average: When the indicator rises above its moving average, it signifies a continued upward movement by the indicator; when the indicator falls below its moving average, it signifies a continued downward movement by the indicator."[4]

Indeed, many and varied are the uses for moving averages, whether used on prices or technical indicators of prices. In this book, we will concentrate primarily on price-only simple moving averages of short-term and intermediate-term time frames.

Moving Average Time Frames	
Trend	**Moving Average**
Very Short Term	5-13 days
Short Term	14-25 days
Minor Intermediate	26-49 days
Intermediate	50-100 days
Long Term	100-200 days

NOTES

1 Achelis, Steven, *Technical Analysis From A to Z*, McGraw
  Hill, 1996, pg. 184

2 Ibid, pg. 184

3 Ibid, pg. 184

4 Ibid, pgs. 184-186

CHAPTER 2

The Benefits of Using Moving Averages:
Spotting Trend Changes and Trading Signals

Price movements of all actively traded securities are a measure of volatility and therefore take on the appearance of being very erratic. To the untrained eye, the price chart of any given security resembles an indecipherable mess of squiggly lines with little meaning. Even to an experienced chart analyst price fluctuations can be very misleading. What is called for in order to eliminate these wild undulations and to enable the analyst to identify the underlying trend is a smoothing device, something to reduce the undulations and isolate the overall movement of prices. This is the function best served by moving averages.

All averages of prices tend to fluctuate less actively than the prices from which they are derived: the greater the number of days from which an average is composed, the more gentle and gradual are the fluctuations relative to the price action from which it is derived.[1]

The moving average is a smoothing device—something to reduce the undulations and isolate the overall movement of prices—which enables an analyst to identify the underlying trend.

In his book, *Commodity Futures Trading With Moving Averages*, J.R. Maxwell provides a succinct account of the usefulness of moving averages when incorporated in a trading program: "The use of an average eliminates or reduces the distraction caused by the often sudden and relatively far-reaching daily price fluctuations, enabling the user to observe a smoother depiction of the trend changes as they occur. This is one of the two principal reasons for the widespread use of various types of averages as trading tools.

The moving average is one of the most versatile and widely used of all technical indicators. Because of the way it is constructed and the fact that it can be so easily quantified and tested, it is the basis for most mechanical trend-following systems in use today.

"The second principal reason is that these figures, when plotted as lines on charts, with the closing prices or other lines representing price action, will cross above and below one another as market trends change. Two averages encompassing different numbers of price units (days) will cross over and under each other in the same fashion. Such crossings, either by themselves, or in combination with other signals, such as changes in statistical data concerning supply and demand, serve as trading signals for a large proportion of the people who speculate in the futures markets.

"These crossings are definite, easily observed signals in a fast-moving and frequently very confusing swirl of activity. Clear-cut signs, such as these are, to buy and to sell, can be comforting to have under such conditions, especially when they appear to be well accepted by so many traders, and their use seems to be based upon solid logic."[2]

The different forms of analysis involving moving averages are many and varied. Many traders place heavy emphasis on the trading signals provided when two moving averages of the underlying security's priceline cross. Others rely on a system involving a moving average or series of moving averages calculated from a moving average itself in relation to the underlying security's price to generate trading signals. Others still prefer to rely simply on a single moving average, which is plotted with the priceline. The results they obtain trading with these signals vary depending on the time frame of the averages used along with a variety of other factors.

Concludes Maxwell: "A moving average is like any tool. It is essential to know its capabilities and its limitations before its potential value can be determined. Then, if it has any merit, skill may be required to obtain the maximum benefit from its use."[3] (For a more detailed discussion of moving average crossovers, please see Chapter 4.)

When used properly and carefully tested, moving averages can act as a tool — generating trading signals — that confirm and forecast turning points in market trends.

NOTES

1 Maxwell, J.R., *Commodity Futures Trading With Moving Averages*, Speer Books, 1976, pg. 5

2 Ibid, pgs. 5-6

3 Ibid, pg. 6

CHAPTER 3

Trading With Single Moving Averages:
A Simple Strategy That Works

One of the most basic, yet proven, techniques for using moving averages as a trading tool is the single moving average method. This trading method involves nothing more than a single, simple moving average of any given length (but preferably suited to the contract and time frame being traded) and its relation to the underlying contract's price. Entry and exit signals for trading are provided by how the priceline trades in relation to the moving average — whether above it or below it. Notice should also be given as to whether or not the moving average is rising or falling relative to the priceline.

Stan Weinstein, editor of the highly regarded *Professional Tape Reader*, is especially noted for his use of this technique. In his book, *Secrets for Profiting in Bull and Bear Markets*, he reveals his preferred method of using moving averages as a timing tool:

"A very important technical tool that helps alert you to both shorter- and longer-term moves [is the moving average]. All that a moving average really

The single moving average method involves nothing more than a single, simple moving average of any given length — preferably suited to the contract and time frame being traded — and its relation to the underlying contract's price.

does is smooth out the major trend so the wild day-to-day gyrations — which the new buying and selling programs have made even wilder — do not throw off your market perspective. Over the years, I've found that a 30-week moving average (MA) is the best one for long-term investors, while the 10-week MA is best for traders to use. A 30-week MA is simply the closing price for this Friday night added to the prior 29 Friday weekly closings. Divide that figure by 30 and the answer is what's plotted on this week's chart.[1] Stocks trading beneath their 30-week MAs should never be considered for purchase, especially if the MA is declining. Stocks trading above their 30-week MAs should never be considered for short selling, especially if the MA is rising. For a long-term investor, the ideal time to buy a stock is when it breaks out above resistance and also moves above its 30-week MA, which must no longer be declining. For a trader who wants action, the ideal time to buy a stock is when it's already above its 30-week MA, when the MA is rising. The trader's ideal entry point is after a stock consolidates in a new trading range and pulls back close to the moving average, then breaks out again above resistance."[2]

Weinstein gives preference to the 50-day (or 10-week) moving average in his analysis of the intermediate cycle, but we prefer the 30-day moving average for short-term trading since it provides faster signals. In the pages that follow, we provide several examples of the use of the simple 30-day and 30-week moving averages using Weinstein's technique for entry and exit.

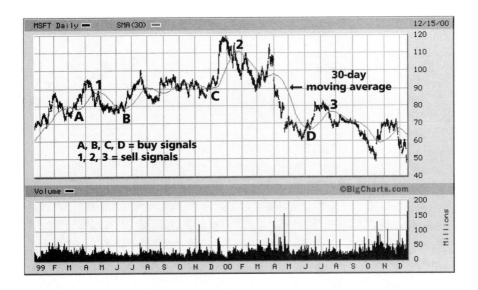

Figure 3-1.   Microsoft (MSFT)

A fine example of a daily chart with a 30-day moving average is Microsoft. Here, the moving average gave decisive buy signals in April, July and December 1999, and in June 2000. Clear-cut sell signals were flashed in May 1999, January 2000, and July 2000. Pay close attention to how the moving average line behaved relative to the priceline at each of these points. Note that before a decisive buy signal is given, the moving average must be in transition from falling to rising, which typically produces a small bowl-shaped formation. This is a strong signal that the short-term cycle has bottomed and that prices will be carried higher. Remember, too, that for a moving average to give a buy signal it must be in an overall rising position, and the priceline should be *above* the average. The reverse is true for a sell signal.

FIGURE 3-1: Daily chart with 30-day moving average.

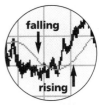

In order for a decisive buy signal to be given, the moving average must be in transition from falling to rising, which typically produces a small bowl-shaped formation.

Figure 3-2. IBM (IBM)

IBM's daily chart with 30-day moving average demonstrates nicely the utility of the MA trading system. Note the buy signals given between April and May 1999 as well as in December 1999, along with sell signals in February 1999, August-September 1999, and February 2000. After the sell signal in February 2000, IBM proceeded to fluctuate rather violently between $100 and $128. However, when the priceline gets too far ahead of the moving average, it is a good idea to ignore the buy signal until prices get back in line with the average and a relative balance has been achieved, and a decisive breakout is made in either direction. This buy signal was given August 2000 near $110. Note how the moving average acted to contain the priceline and provided strong support at this area. When this happens it is an emphatic indication that prices are going higher. The next sell signal was flashed a

FIGURE 3-2: Daily chart with 30-day moving average.

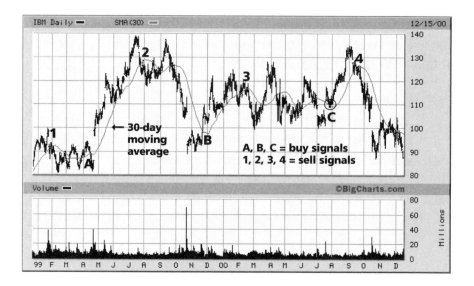

MOVING AVERAGES SIMPLIFIED

Note how the moving average acted to contain the priceline and provided strong support at this area. When this happens it is an emphatic indication that prices are going higher.

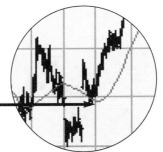

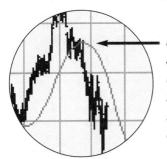

Note how the MA lost momentum and curved over as the priceline slid underneath. A downward curving moving average is a sign of not only lost momentum but of a peak in the dominant cycle as well.

Entry and exit signals for trading are provided by how the priceline trades in relation to the moving average — whether above it or below it. Notice should also be given as to whether or not the moving average is rising or falling relative to the priceline.

month later in September 2000 near $130. Note how the MA lost momentum and curved over as the priceline slid underneath. A downward curving moving average is a sign of not only lost momentum but of a peak in the dominant cycle as well.

Figure 3-3.   General Motors (GM)

Here is a fine instance of a fast-moving stock in General Motors. There are many excellent profit opportunities in seasoned, closely held stocks such as this one. Note the sell signal given in May 1999, and the buy signals given in November 1999 and August 2000. Only at one point in November 1999 was a decisive buy signal given, despite many false starts between July and September of that year. That is because at this point the priceline moved decisively higher as the moving average also turned

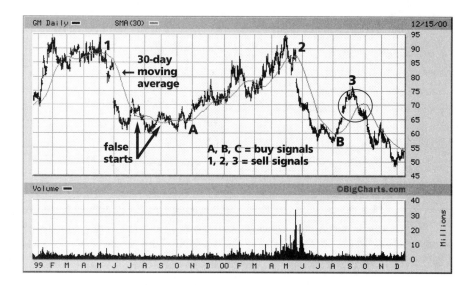

**FIGURE 3-3:
Daily chart with
30-day moving
average.**

up. Remember our rule: prices must be above the
rising moving average before buying. The trader
who followed blindly these rules would have gotten
out too late in September 2000; however, the dis-
cerning trader would have noted that prices got
too far out of line with the moving average in the
circled area and would have taken profits before
the next sell-off. Remember: whenever the priceline
gets too far away from the moving averages, it's
time to sell.

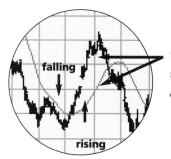

*Whenever the priceline gets
too far away from the moving
averages, it's time to sell.*

Figure 3-4.   J.P. Morgan (JPM)

A buy signal between February and March 1999 carried J.P. Morgan to significantly higher levels until the first decisive sell signal was given in June 1999 near the $135 area. [Even though the moving average flattened out early in 1999 around the $105 level it never actually began falling; thus, the trader should have held his long position in JPM.] Another buy signal was flashed in October 1999 near the $100 area (note price spike and corresponding dip in the MA); however, this was a steep but short-lived run as the priceline got too far above its moving average, warning the trader to sell. Yet another buy signal was given in March 2000 near the $100 level, and yet again the priceline carried too far away from its MA, warning the trader that supply and demand were getting out of balance. The trader who bought in at the next buy signal in July 2000 between $130-$135

FIGURE 3-4: Daily chart with 30-day moving average.

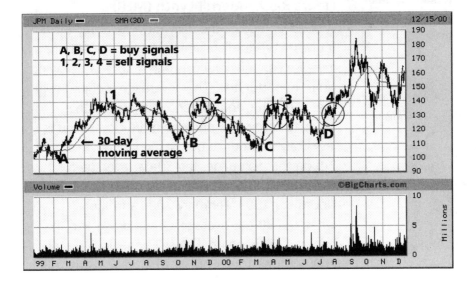

Safety should be the first considera-
tion in any moving average trading
system. Note behavior of MA in
this area relative to the priceline.
This premonitory sell signal is a
"heads up" to sell at the first avail-
ble opportunity.

When the price-line gets too far ahead of the moving average, it is a good idea to ignore the buy signal until prices get back in line with the average and a relative balance has been achieved, and a decisive breakout is made in either direction.

(note behavior of MA in this area relative to the priceline) was given a premonitory sell signal in September near the $155-$160 zone as the price-line carried too far ahead of the moving average. This gave him a "heads up" to sell at the first available opportunity. While JPM went on to rise even higher, it later crashed without warning. Safety should be the first consideration in any moving average trading system.

Figure 3-5. Merrill Lynch (MER)

A disadvantage of the daily moving average is that it gives more trading signals, which if acted on, increase commission costs and reduce large-swing profit opportunities. The advantage it enjoys over the weekly moving average, however, is that it tends to follow the priceline more closely and is less likely to produce devastating losses. In Figure 3-5 on the next page, the 30-day average for Merrily Lynch gives buy signals in March 1999, November 1999, February 2000 and June 2000, when the 30-day average turned down and the priceline fell beneath it. A sell signal in September 2000 got the trader out just before a major sell-

A, B, C, D = buy signals
1, 2, 3, 4 = sell signals

30-day
moving
average

Volume ▬   ©BigCharts.com

off. Note how the priceline bounced off the moving average in March of that year. Again, this indicates strong support and is an indication that prices are likely going higher in the near future.

FIGURE 3-5:
Daily chart with
30-day moving
average.

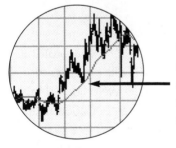

Note how the priceline bounces off the moving average. This shows strong support and is an indication that prices are likely going higher in the near future.

Figure 3-6.   Sears (S)

Buy signals for Sears were flashed in March and November 1999, and in April and September 2000 on the daily chart. The sell signals were given in June 1999, February 2000, and June 2000. Also note the higher lows in the moving average between April and September 2000—a bullish indication. Notice also the

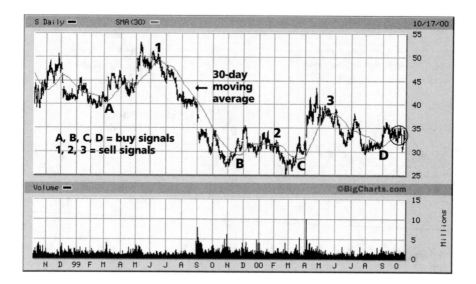

**FIGURE 3-6:
Daily chart with
30-day moving
average.**

activity near the $30-$35 area in October 2000. This fluctuation around the moving average near a low in Sears' chart provides a strong indication that prices are headed higher over the near term.

Figure 3-7. XAU Gold Silver Index

Compare both the daily and the weekly charts of the XAU gold/silver index, Figure 3-7. Notice how in the daily chart (top) decisive buy signals were flashed in April 1999, August 1999, and December 2000. The sell signals were given in June 1999 and October 1999. Also note the distinct "head and shoulders" bottom pattern that formed between August 2000 and January 2001. At the "head" part of the pattern notice how the 30-day moving average made a deep bowl-shaped dip then bounced higher. This is a sign that the XAU's dominant intermediate-term cycle has bottomed and that the new trend is for higher prices. The bullish head and shoulders pattern confirms this

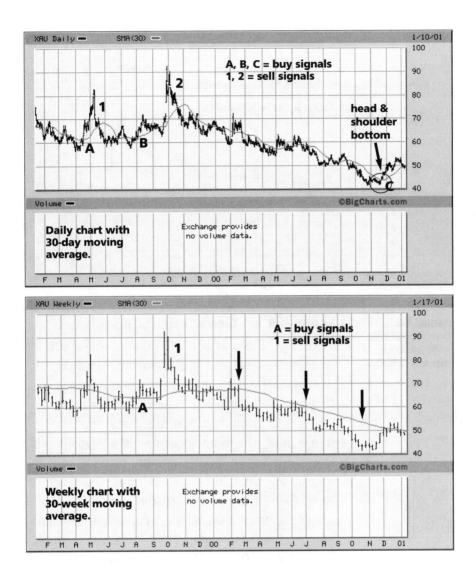

FIGURE 3-7: TOP: Daily chart with 30-day moving average. BOTTOM: Weekly chart with 30-week moving average.

reading. On the weekly chart however, the only decisive buy signal given was in April 1999, followed by a sell signal in October of the same year. From that point on, the 30-week moving average acted as resistance, keeping the priceline from rising above the moving average line.

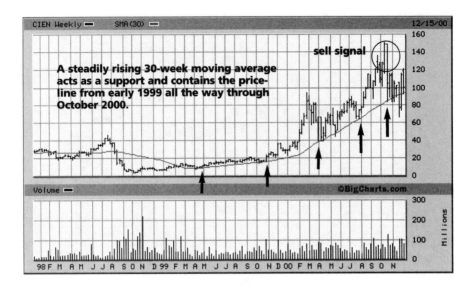

A steadily rising 30-week moving average acts as a support and contains the price-line from early 1999 all the way through October 2000.

sell signal

©BigCharts.com

FIGURE 3-8:
Weekly chart
with 30-week
moving average.

Figure 3-8.   Ciena Corp. (CIEN)

We now turnour attention to the weekly chart and the 30-week moving average. Once again we discover the advantages of using a longer time frame chart in our moving average analysis. This is due to the fact that the longer the time frame used, the more accurate our analysis is likely to be, due to the greater amount of price and volume information contained within the chart. Here, Ciena Corp. saw a steadily rising 30-week moving average that acted to beautifully contain the priceline from early 1999 all the way through the October 2000. At this point the priceline plunged beneath the MA, and the MA itself is starting to curve over, indicative of waning momentum. Traders should have exited long positions in Ciena at the first sign of trouble in the fall of 2000.

Figure 3-9. Citigroup (C)

Citigroup gave a decisive buy signal in February 1998, but notice how the priceline quickly got out of line with the moving average, moving considerably above it. The high volume one-week reversal in April would have been a good place to exit long positions in anticipation of a sell-off. This is why it is important to watch not only the moving average line, but the priceline and the volume bars as well to see how each interact with one another. None of these three elements can be ignored or studied separately but must be analyzed in relation to each other. A sell signal was formally flashed in August 1998, with the next buy signal coming in March 1999. Note how the moving average contained the priceline slide and acted as support one month earlier in February. This was a clue to the alert trader that the trend was still up. By November 2000,

It is important to watch not only the moving average line, but the priceline and the volume bars as well to see how each interact with one another.

FIGURE 3-9: Weekly chart with 30-week moving average.

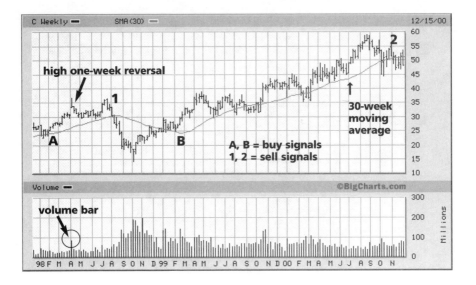

the moving average had lost momentum and was giving a warning that the trend was in transition from up to down. Conservative traders would have sold at this point.

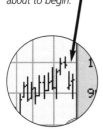

FIGURE 3-10: Weekly chart with 30-week moving average.

Figure 3-10. Cardinal Healt (CAH)

Here is another great example of how a single average trading system can serve as a profitable tool for selling short. In this example, note how conspicuously the priceline for Cardinal Health moves away from its 30-week moving average between May and November of 2000. Even though traders had no way of knowing when the run up would end, they knew it would end in violent fashion based on the extreme distance between the priceline and the MA. A breakaway gap appeared the first week in December, cluing the trader that the sell-off was about to begin.

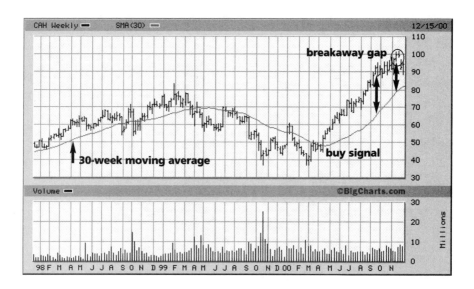

As we have seen, using simple moving averages can help us determine how to pinpoint entry and exit points. Now let's turn our attention to how to use two moving averages for the same purpose.

NOTES

1 A 10-week MA is obviously this Friday's closing price for a given stock added to the prior nine Friday closings and then divided by 10.

2 Weinstein, Stan., *Secrets for Profiting in Bull and Bear Markets*, McGraw Hill, 1988, pg. 13-14.

CHAPTER 4

Trading With Two Moving Averages
What They Are and How to Use Them
for High-Impact Results

Using two moving averages—one of shorter length and one of longer length—to generate trading signals is commonly used among traders today. This method, known as the "double crossover method," is especially suited for securities that happen to be in trending, as opposed to range-bound, markets. (Trending markets are characterized by steady upward price movement in bull markets and steady downward price movement in bear markets. Prolonged sideways movement with little sustained progress up or down is characteristic of "range bound" markets.)

There are many different ways in which this double crossover method may be used. The combination possibilities are endless. The two moving averages can be daily or weekly, but one must always be of a shorter time frame than the other. For example, you might consider using a 12- and 24-day moving average in conjunction with a security's price chart. Or a 10- and 30-day, or (as in the chart examples

The double crossover method is the use of two moving averages —one of shorter length and one of longer length— to generate trading signals.

we provide here, a 30-day and 60-day average). The shorter moving average measures the short-term trend, while the longer MA measures the longer-term trend. Buying and selling signals are given whenever the two cross over or under one another.

Trading rules for the double crossover method are quite simple: whenever the shorter-term moving average crosses above the longer-term moving average—and the longer-term MA happens to be rising—a buy signal is generated. Conversely, whenever the shorter-term average falls beneath the longer-term average—and the longer-term average happens to be falling—a sell signal is generated.

BigCharts.com provides a free charting service through its Internet site (www.bigcharts.com), which contains charting tools for constructing several varieties of moving averages. The daily and weekly bar charts on the BigCharts.com Web site can be modified to the time frame that best suits the trader. Included in this chapter are a number of BigCharts.com stock charts, and the buy or sell signals they generated based on the crossover method using the 30-day and 60-day moving average. Bear in mind that the same rules that apply for interpreting the 30-day and 60-day moving average combo apply for all types of double series moving averages; and can be used for all time frames, including daily, weekly and monthly charts.

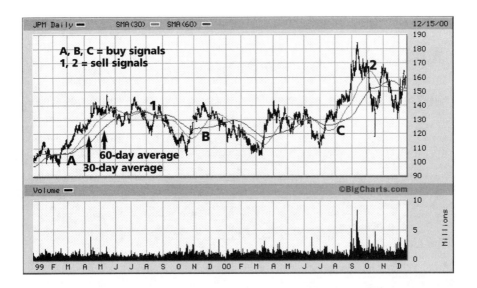

A, B, C = buy signals
1, 2 = sell signals

60-day average
30-day average

JPM Daily ▬   SMA(30) ▬ SMA(60) ▬   12/15/00

Volume ▬

Figure 4-1.   J.P. Morgan (JPM)

Here is a fine example of how the double crossover system of moving averages works in J.P. Morgan. Here, the daily chart provides a buy signal when the shorter 30-day moving average crosses over the longer 60-day moving average. Conversely, a sell signal is flashed when the longer of the two averages (60-day) crosses over and remains on top of the shorter average (30-day). This basic rule of thumb applies for moving averages of any size and not just the 30-day and 60-day functions. Notice in March 1999 that the first buy signal was given as the 30-day average (light-colored line) crossed on top of the darker 60-day line. So long as the price bars were rising and remained on top of the averages, the buy signal remained intact. This was the case from March through June 1999, at which point the priceline dropped underneath the averages and the averages started turning down, indi-

FIGURE 4-1: Daily two-year bar chart with 30-day and 60-day moving averages.

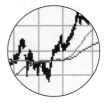

A buy signal is generated whenever the shorter-term moving average crosses above the longer-term moving average—and the longer-term MA happens to be rising.

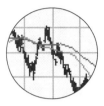

A sell signal is generated whenever the shorter-term average falls beneath the longer-term average—and the longer-term average happens to be falling.

cating a loss of momentum. In August 1999 the 60-day average crossed on top of the 30-day average, flashing a sell signal. This continued until November, when another buy signal occurred. However, since the two moving averages got so far out of synch with one another, it warned the trader to avoid making a commitment to the stock until the averages got back in line. The next "in-line" buy signal occurred in August 2000 (note how the two averages interacted at this time on the chart). Because the two averages became widely spaced apart shortly after this signal, it indicated that an over-bought condition was developing in J.P. Morgan. Therefore, the prudent trader would have been right to look for exit signals. The first such signal came in October, at which time the 30-day average turned down and failed to support the priceline. Even though a crossover did not occur until one month later, it would have been wise to sell out when first the 30-day moving average turned down. The rules for interpreting single line moving averages still apply when interpreting double line moving averages, even when the two lines have not yet crossed over.

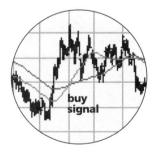

Even though a buy signal is generated, note how the two moving averages are so far out of synch with one another—a warning to avoid making a commitment to the stock until the averages get back in line.

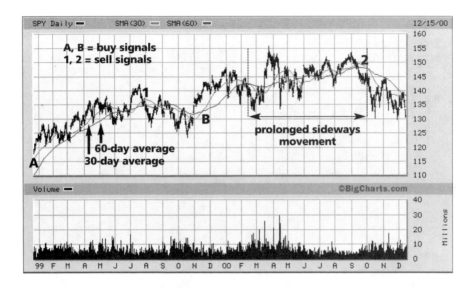

SPY Daily ▬   SMA(30) ▬ SMA(60) ▬   12/15/00

A, B = buy signals
1, 2 = sell signals

60-day average
30-day average

prolonged sideways movement

Volume ▬   ©BigCharts.com

Figure 4-2.
Standard & Poor's Depository Receipts (SPY)

A buy signal in the Standard & Poor's Depository Receipts (SPY) remained in place throughout 1999 until August of that year until the two moving averages starting rounding off and turning down. Shortly thereafter, a bearish crossover occurred, though it would have been wise to exit long positions as soon as the moving averages—particularly the 30-day average—starting curving over, reflecting waning momentum. Another strong buy signal was given in November 1999, when the 30-day average crossed through the 60-day average. It soon starting curving over, however, and the priceline began a prolonged sideways movement into the year 2000. The next formal sell signal was flashed in September, at which time the 60-day average crossed over the 30-day average. The sell signal remained in place through the remainder of the year.

FIGURE 4-2:
Daily two-year bar chart with 30-day and 60-day moving averages.

Even though a crossover did not occur until one month later, the safest exit point was to sell when the moving averages started curving over.

FIGURE 4-3:
Daily two-year
bar chart with
30-day and
60-day moving
averages.

Figure 4-3. General Motors (GM)

General Motors provides a clear sell signal in its
daily chart in May 1999 (note crossover and downward curve of moving averages and their relation to
the priceline). A buy signal was given in October
1999 (note bowl-shaped bottoming pattern of moving averages, the rising priceline in relation to the rising averages and the crossover of the shorter average (30-day) on top of the longer average (60-day).
The next sign of trouble came in May 2000, when
the two averages got out of line with both curving
over. The priceline plunged through both of them
before bouncing higher. This should have been the
trader's warning signal to exit all long positions in
GM and sell the stock short. Remember, when trading using two moving averages, you do not necessarily have to await a crossover before making a
trading commitment—a simple curve of one or both
of the moving averages, or a failure of the moving

averages to contain the priceline is all the signal that is required. The crossover serves more or less as a confirmation to the preliminary buy or sell signal.

Figure 4-4. DuPont (DD)

Here is a daily chart of DuPont (DD), a leading industrial stock and a component of the Dow Jones Industrial Average. A strong buy signal was given in April 1999, when both moving averages were close together and moved up at the same time while the price bars were also rising. A separation of the two averages occurred between May and June of that year, followed by a curving over of the shorter (30-day) moving average in June. This provided a preliminary sell signal to the alert trader. An all-out sell signal was given in September when the 30-day average fell below the falling 60-day average. This was followed by falling prices and then a short-term buy signal in December 1999. However, notice that in

A preliminary sell signal is given when the moving averages begin to separate, followed by a curving over of one or both of them. The crossover serves more or less as a confirmation to the preliminary buy signal.

FIGURE 4-4: Daily two-year bar chart with 30-day and 60-day moving averages.

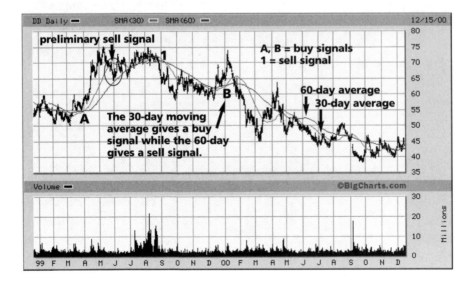

Remember, when trading using two moving averages, you do not necessarily have to await a crossover before making a trading commitment—a simple curve of one or both of the moving averages, or a failure of the moving averages to contain the priceline is all the signal that is required.

the month between December 1999 and January 2000, even as DuPont's priceline was moving higher, the 30-day moving average ascended while the 60-day average never followed suit. Instead, the 60-day moving average, after a short rise in December, quickly turned back down and continued to curve lower even as the 30-day average was rising. This is what is known as a divergence, and it is typically bearish. In cases like these where one moving average gives a buy signal while the other gives a sell signal, it is best to exit long positions and either await a clearer signal before re-establishing trading positions or else sell short (if you are an aggressive trader). The longer of the two averages holds more significance, so in this case the fact that the 60-day average was falling implied that the longer-term trend was still down; therefore, short positions were justified. The sell-off continued throughout the year 2000; however, notice how the two averages had moved close together and were starting to round off in bowl fashion. This provides a clue that the sell-off likely has halted and that accumulation could be underway. The trader should watch this chart carefully in anticipation of the next buy signal.

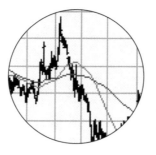

This example illustrates divergence — the priceline moved higher, the 30-day moving average ascended while the 60-day average never followed suit. Instead, the 60-day moving average turned back down and continued to curve lower even as the 30-day average was rising.

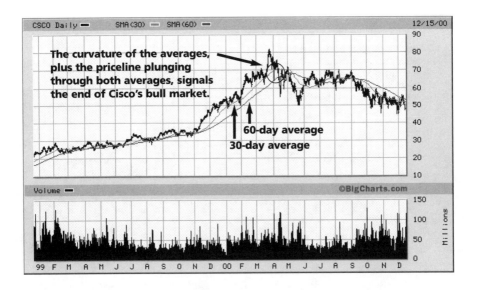

The curvature of the averages, plus the priceline plunging through both averages, signals the end of Cisco's bull market.

60-day average
30-day average

CSCO Daily ▬   SMA(30) ▬   SMA(60) ▬   12/15/00

Volume ▬   ©BigCharts.com

Figure 4-5.   Cisco Systems (CSCO)

A bullish buy signal continued throughout 1999 and into the early part of 2000. Notice, however, that the moving averages began moving apart in early 2000 and continued to spread apart into April, at which time the 30-day moving average started to curve over with the 60-day average soon following suit. The first sell signal was given in April when the price-line for Cisco Systems fell through both averages. Although there was a quick bounce back, the curvature of the averages plus the fact that the priceline had previously plunged through them, was strong evidence that Cisco's bull market had ended and that further weakness could be expected.

Figure 4-6.   Chinadotcom Corp. (CHINA)

The chart provided on the next page for Chinadotcom Corp. (CHINA) is a great example of how a

FIGURE 4-5:
Daily two-year bar chart with 30-day and 60-day moving averages.

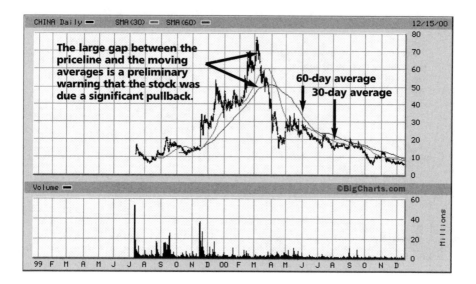

The large gap between the priceline and the moving averages is a preliminary warning that the stock was due a significant pullback.

60-day average
30-day average

Volume ▬   ©BigCharts.com

FIGURE 4-6: Daily two-year bar chart with 30-day and 60-day moving averages.

moving average system can serve to protect traders from adverse moves in the stock market. After an extraordinary advance from its initial public offering in July 1999, CHINA proceeded to rise to a price of nearly $80 a share in March 2000. The large gap between the priceline and the moving averages that occurred in March 2000 (just before the crash) was a preliminary warning that the stock was due a significant pullback. Although there is no hard-and-fast rule as to just how far the distance between the priceline and moving average should be before a sell signal is given, it is up to the trader to use discretion based on the "average" distance between the two over the long-term. Whenever it becomes plainly evident that there is a wide separation between the moving average and the priceline, the trader should prepare to either sell or sell short. Notice also how both averages — particularly the 60-day average — began losing momentum and curving over just before the sell-off occurred. This was yet another advance warning that a plunge was imminent. After the initial crash, CHINA continued to trade below the two moving averages for the rest of the year, indicating that selling pressure was intense throughout.

Figure 4-7. Boston Properties (BXP)

The chart for Boston Properties (BXP) served as a wonderful guide for making profits over a two-year period. Using the double moving average system, a trader, after initially buying in April 1999, knew to sell short between May and June of that year as the gap between the 30-day and the 60-day moving averages widened conspicuously. The sell signal was confirmed in July as the averages crossed over. The trend remained down until December 1999, at which time a preliminary buy signal was flashed as the two averages bottomed and turned up togeth-

Whenever it becomes plainly evident that there is a wide separation between the moving average and the priceline, the trader should prepare to either sell or sell short.

FIGURE 4-7: Daily two-year bar chart with 30-day and 60-day moving averages.

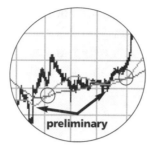

A preliminary buy signal was flashed as the two averages bottomed and turned up together. However, the signal was not confirmed until almost a month later when the 30-day moving average crossed over the 60-day and both turned upward.

preliminary

er (the crossover occurred the next month). After a rocky start in the initial months of 2000, a firm buy signal was flashed in March, and from there prices headed higher. A preliminary sell signal was given in September 2000, as both averages lost momentum and curved over. Although the next firm buy signal had not been given as of December, it was beginning to look like a distinct possibility. Note how both averages are very close together and appear to be turning up with the priceline moving higher. However, as a clear-cut buy signal has not yet been flashed it is safest to remain on the sidelines awaiting a clear signal. Both averages must turn higher before a long position can be safely established.

Moving averages can act as support and resistance for the priceline. Support in the MA is the area where the bottom rounds and turns upward — containing the priceline above it. Resistance is the area where the MA starts to curve over and move downward — keeping the priceline below it.

Figure 4-8.
Resource Asset Investment Trust (RAS)

Resource Asset Investment Trust (RAS) is a dynamic stock that can be traded with wonderful results using a double moving average trading system. Note here the interplay between its 30-day and 60-day moving averages. Note especially how the two lines cross through each other at critical turning points along the timeline. Whenever the 30-day moving averages crosses through and above the rising 60-day average, it always precedes a big run-up in share price. Note also how well the averages tend to act as support and resistance for the price-line. The first significant buy signal came in May 1999 when the 30-day MA crossed through and above the 60-day MA. Both curved over in August, at which point the trader should have sold short. A "rounding" process occurred between November 1999 and July 2000 during which time both the priceline and the averages produced a bowl-shaped curve, implying accumulation was taking place. The next buy signal was finally flashed in July 2000, which saw RAS rocket from its low near $10.50 to a high of nearly $13 in three months — a hefty percentage gain. After a prompt sell-off from the October high, the averages curved over and failed to support the falling priceline, at which time the trader should have sold. By December, however, the

FIGURE 4-8: Daily two-year bar chart with 30-day and 60-day moving averages.

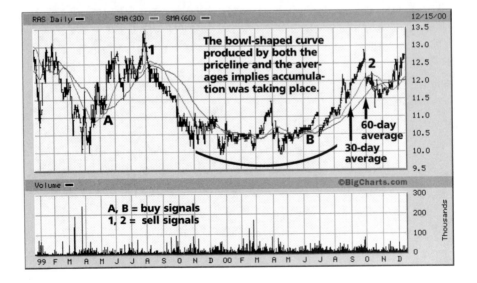

30-day moving average appeared to be ready to cross through the 60-day average, which would send another buy signal.

Let's now move on to chapter five which explains how using moving averages to isolate price cycle bottoms can be a profitable tool for initiating trades.

CHAPTER 5

Using Moving Averages to Identify Price Cycles:

An Important Tool to Discover Profitable Entry Points

Earlier in the book we explained the importance of being able to identify price cycles, particularly cycles of short and intermediate duration. We will now explain how moving averages can greatly aid the trader in isolating these cycle bottoms in order to discover profitable entry points for initiating trades. As you will learn, moving averages serve an extremely important function when it comes to cycle identification. The chart examples in this chapter will serve to illustrate this.

Moving averages can greatly aid the trader in isolating cycle bottoms in order to discover profitable entry points for initiating trades.

In his book, *Technical Analysis of the Futures Markets*, John Murphy makes the following astute observation concerning the relation between cycles and moving averages:

"There appears to be a definite relationship between moving averages and cycles. For example, the monthly cycle is one of the best known cycles operating throughout the commodity markets. A month has 20 to 21 trading days. Cycles tend to be related to their next longer and shorter cycles harmonically, or by a factor of two. That means that the next longer cycle is double the length of a cycle and the next shorter cycle is half its length.

"The monthly cycle, therefore, may explain the popularity of the 5-, 10-, 20-, and 40-day moving averages. The 20-day cycle measures the monthly cycle. The 40-day average is double the 20-day. The 10-day average is half of 20 and the 5-day average is half again of ten.

"Many of the more commonly used moving averages (including the 4-, 9-, and 18-day averages, which are derivatives of five, ten, and 20) can be explained by cycle influences and the harmonic relationships of neighboring cycles."[1]

Using the form of moving average analysis we will advocate in this chapter, we will attempt to locate cycle bottoms using a simple moving average of short or intermediate length. For example, in looking at a one-year daily bar chart of a security, say IBM, we want to isolate when the 3-4 month cycle bottomed each time so that we can find profitable entry and entry points for trading in the company's shares. Using the priceline alone, we sometimes get a misleading picture of where the 3-4 month cycle may have bottomed since sharp reversals in price occasionally occur at intervals less than three months. How, then, do we eliminate this problem? By "smoothing" the priceline with a simple moving average. To isolate the 3-4 month cycle, we have found the 30-day moving average to be the optimal length. All of the examples provided in this chapter involve the 30-day MA.

The interpretation of this method of moving average analysis is quite simple: whenever the 30-day moving average shows a noticeable dip, it strongly implies the 3-4 month cycle has bottomed.

The interpretation of this method of moving average analysis is quite simple: whenever the 30-day MA shows a noticeable dip, it strongly implies the 3-4 month cycle has bottomed. Since a picture is worth a thousand words, we will cease to explain in writing how to interpret this moving average and instead illustrate this method in actual chart examples in the pages that follow.

The more decisive the dip in the moving average, the more likely that the cycle has bottomed strongly and will carry prices considerably higher.

Figure 5-1.   Intel (INTC)

In the daily chart for Intel Corp., a clear-cut bottom in the 3-4 month cycle can be seen in June 1999 (circled), where the 30-day moving average dips, then rises to higher levels. Four months later in November this cycle bottoms again (second circle). The bottom in the 6-8 month cycle occurs in late May/early June as evidenced by the emphatic bowl-shape in the moving average, followed by a rise. The 3-4 month cycle bottoms again in August, but

FIGURE 5-1:
Two-year daily chart with 30-day moving average.

because the dip was shallow and because the MA failed to exceed the previous peak, it provided an indication that Intel was in a weak position and should therefore have been sold. The more decisive the dip in the moving average, the more likely that the cycle has bottomed strongly and will carry prices considerably higher.

Figure 5-2.   Microsoft (MSFT)

A clear 3-month cycle can be seen in this daily chart of Microsoft. Note the first three dips in the 30-day moving average (first three circles), each of which is spaced at a 3-month interval. The next 3-month cycle bottom occurred in late March 2000, but since the dip in the 30-day MA was so shallow, and since the ensuing rise in Microsoft's stock price was so out of line relative to the MA, the trader could surmise that the bounce in price would not last and should

**FIGURE 5-2:
Two-year daily
chart with 30-day
moving average.**

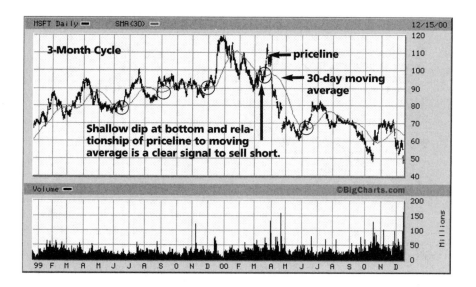

have sold short. The next bottom in the 3-month price cycle occurred in June 2000 (circled). When the priceline plunged beneath the 30-day average, the trader should have sold once again.

Figure 5-3.   Johnson and Johnson (JNJ)

Johnson and Johnson's daily chart provides many strong indications of changes in the 3-4 and 6-8 month cycles based on a reading of the 30-day moving average. Note the first such bottom in January 1999 (circled area). This was followed by a strong move into July of that year, at which time the 6-month cycle bottomed (circled). The 4-month cycle then bottomed in October that same year, followed by another bottom in the 6-month cycle in April 2000. The next bottom in the 6-month cycle should occur sometime in October-November 2000, and long commitments in this stock should be avoided until the cycle shows signs of having bottomed.

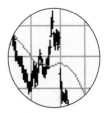

An extremely shallow dip, coupled with a priceline that rises too far away from the moving average line, is an advanced warning to sell.

FIGURE 5-3: Two-year daily chart with 30-day moving average.

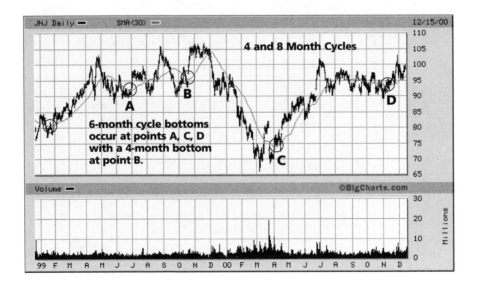

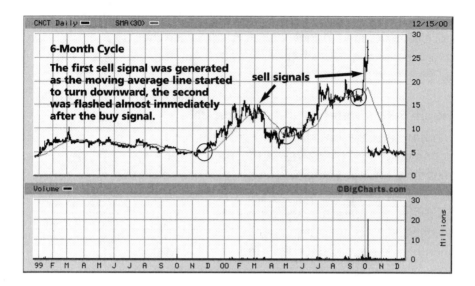

6-Month Cycle

The first sell signal was generated as the moving average line started to turn downward, the second was flashed almost immediately after the buy signal.

sell signals →

©BigCharts.com

Volume ▬

Millions

99 F M A M J J A S O N D 00 F M A M J J A S O N D

FIGURE 5-4:
Two-year daily chart with 30-day moving average.

Figure 5-4.   Connetics Corp. (CNCT)

The daily chart for Connetics Corp. is a study in how moving averages can help the trader avoid disaster. A clear-cut cycle bottom was seen on the chart in late November 1999 (circled). This carried prices higher into March, at which time the 30-day moving average turned down and flashed a sell signal. The next cycle bottom — as evidenced by the dip in the 30-day MA between May and June — provided another buy signal, which again saw prices climb considerably higher. However, an extremely shallow

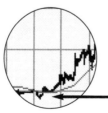
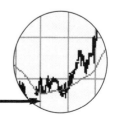

Buy signals are generated at cycle bottoms — the stronger the dip the more decisive the buy signal.

dip in the 30-day MA in September 2000 (circled), coupled with the fact that Connetics' priceline rose too far and too rapidly away form the moving average, provided the trader with advanced warning that a crash was in store for Connetics. The trader should have sold short.

Figure 5-5. Ford (F)

The first emphatic buy signal in this daily chart for Ford Motor Co. wasn't flashed until September 1999. However, the trader should have sold in November based on the sell signal provided by the 30-day moving average. From here, the 6-month cycle ran its course until late March 2000, at which time the next buy signal was given.

**FIGURE 6-5:
Two-year daily
chart with 30-day
moving average.**

Next, we will move on to a more detailed discussion of price cycle identification and how this tool can be used to enhance trading success.

NOTES

1 Murphy, John, *Technical Analysis of the Futures Markets*, New York Institute of Finance, 1986, pgs. 259-260

CHAPTER 6

Principle of Threeness and Fourness:
How Price Cycle Repetition Creates
Opportunities for Traders

While many things have been written on the subject of moving averages, most of the current literature on this useful technical tool has centered on its use as either a directional indicator, an isolator of support and resistance, an entry/exit pinpointer, or some combination of each of these. And while a moving average or combination of averages—with the properly chosen time frame—have been known to fill each of these roles admirably, it is to another purpose that we dedicate this book. It is our belief that the most useful role of the moving average is that of price cycle bottom identifier. To that end, we will focus most of our energies in explaining this extremely important role the MA plays.

Cycles —that rhythmic fluctuation from one high to a corresponding low over a period of time — govern the movements of all prices and moving averages are nothing more than a reflection of these underlying price cycles.

One can hardly enter upon the subject of moving averages without first discussing price cycles. For it is cycles that govern the movements of all prices, and moving averages are nothing more than a reflection of these underlying price cycles.

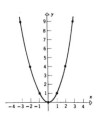

Most cycle experts agree the parabola is the geometric form that best captures the essence of the cycle.

But what are these cycles? A cycle is properly defined as the displacement of an object returning to its point of origin.[1] In simple language, this means that any given commodity can be expected to alternate from one price to the next in a fairly regular, rhythmic fashion, and that the price will (in any free, unencumbered market) never maintain an equilibrium at a set level, but will fluctuate from one high to a corresponding low over a period of time. The best way to envision a cycle is to imagine a parabola (which most cycle experts agree is the geometric form that best captures the essence of the cycle).

In the charts, the cycle manifests most commonly in the form of a bottom or top reversal pattern, particularly the "V-top" or "V-bottom" reversal, so named because of its shape. Notice the example in the chart that follows below (see Figure 6-1).

**FIGURE 6-1:
IBM daily chart
with a 30-day
moving avearge.**

Note here the strong cycle bottoms that occurred in the daily chart for IBM in 1998. Note especially the

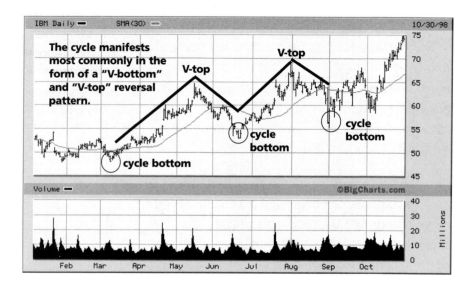

V-bottom in the priceline that occurred in March, which was confirmed by the moving average providing support for the priceline along the way after the reversal. Note also the V-top reversal in May of that year, at which point the trader should have sold IBM short. Another sign that the cycle had topped out for IBM was the fact that the 30-day moving average was too far out of line with the priceline and was beginning to turn over. Yet another cycle bottom occurred in June and another in September. This equates to a regularly recurring 3-month cycle in IBM.

In order to gain a clearer conception of cycles, and to further us along to our goal of understanding moving averages, we will examine the basics of cycle analysis. One of the most basic assumptions underlying cycle analysis is what we will call the "Principle of Threeness and Fourness." This principle, the discovery of the great cycle analyst P.Q. Wall [2], will provide a most excellent starting point to our study of cycles, and by extension, moving averages. In a nutshell, this principle states that cycles of all magnitudes and durations can be expected to conform to some derivative of the numbers three or four. Under this principle there are four families of cycles worth noting: the 3-4 week cycle; the 3-4 month cycle; the 6-8 month cycle (double the 3-4 month cycle); and the 3-4 year cycle (i.e., Kitchin or "Business" Cycle). This prime family of cycles manifest in nearly every actively traded security, including stocks, stock indexes, bonds, commodities, and currencies. It is remarkable indeed to watch as these basic cycles appear over and over in the charts that are included in this chapter.

"Principle of Threeness and Fourness" states that cycles of all magnitudes and durations can be expected to conform to some derivative of the numbers three or four. Under this principle there are four families of cycles worth noting:
- **3-4 week cycle**
- **3-4 month cycle**
- **6-8 month cycle**
- **3-4 year cycle**

Before going any further, keep in mind that cycles are "fixed" as opposed to dynamic. What this means is that the price fluctuations for a given stock or commodity, say the Dow Jones Industrial Average, are governed by cycles which cannot be changed or altered. So, for instance, the 3-4 month cycle can be a 3-month cycle for one security or commodity and a 4-month cycle for another, but never can the two cycles alternate in a given stock or commodity. One of the two cycles governs the stock or commodity in question, but not both. The Dow's dominant short-term cycle is the 4-month cycle, therefore it is correct to say that the Dow has a 4-month cycle rhythm. It would be incorrect to say that the Dow had a 3-4 month cycle rhythm as the cycles cannot alternate (see Figure 6-2).

This same concept of unchangeable cycles is true for the 3-4 week cycle, the 6-8 month cycle, the 3-4 year cycle, the 6-8 year cycle, etc. For example, a stock or commodity can have a 6-month rhythm as its dominant intermediate-term cycle, or a 7-month rhythm, or an 8-month rhythm, but not all three. This is what we mean by 6-8 month cycle.

From this starting point, then, we may proceed to applying our knowledge of these cycles and learn to identify them on the chart. But how are these cycles measured? Cycle analysts are often at odds as to how to go about counting cycles. Many believe cycles should be counted strictly on a time basis without reference to price and volume patterns on the chart. Others (this author included) insist that cycles should only be analyzed with respect to obvious manifestations on the chart. How this is accomplished will be explained in the pages that follow.

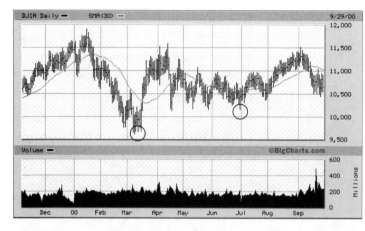

FIGURE 6-2:
4-month cycle
bottoms for
Dow Jones

Dow Jones
Industrials

Dow Jones
Transports

Dow Jones
Utilities

Identification of Cycle Bottoms

The most important facet of all forms of cycle analysis involves the identification of cycle bottoms. By "bottoms," we are referring to the temporary reversals of a downward trend that occur periodically. Isolating these reversals, or cycle bottoms, on a chart is easy once you've acquired the knack. Such sharp (in most cases), sudden reversals of trend tend to occur on high volume, although this is not always the case. Nevertheless, looking for conspicuous spikes in trading volume will often serve to confirm a cycle bottom. (See Figure 6-3). Moving averages can help the trader in this regard since a cycle bottom will always be accompanied by the bowl-shaped dip in the moving average line; conversely, a cycle top will be accompanied by a dome-shaped turnover in the moving average line. In fact, moving averages serve the function of distilling the cycle—whichever cycle you happen to be following. However, you

FIGURE 6-3: Huffy Corp. daily chart with a 30-day moving average.

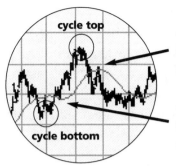

A cycle top will be accompanied by a dome-shaped turnover in the moving average line.

A cycle bottom will always be accompanied by the bowl-shaped dip in the moving average line.

must experiment with different moving average time frames in order to capture the tops and bottoms in these cycles. For instance, we recommend using the 30-day moving average for detecting turns in the 3-4 week and 3-4 month cycle, while the 30-week moving average works best for identifying turns in the 6-8 month cycle.

Identifying 3-4 Month Cycles

Figure 6-1, on page 60, and Figure 6-2, on page 63, are good examples of price reversals occurring at 3-month and 4-month intervals. While there is no precision in predicting exactly when the 3-4 month cycle may bottom, it may be inferred by counting the cycles in whatever chart you happen to be looking at—since each chart has its own unique rhythm. For instance, a chart for the Swiss Franc futures contract (not shown) may tend to favor a 4-month-type cycle while a chart for corn futures (not shown) may favor a 3-month-type cycle. While this is not an infallible guide to predicting when a cycle may bottom, it is nevertheless helpful to keep this in mind.

In fact, the average for the 3-4 month cycle across all actively traded stocks and commodities is 3$\frac{1}{3}$ months, which equates roughly to 13 weeks. Silver futures, for example, typically trade in a predictable 13-week cycle. It is up to you as the trader to determine the long-term average of the intermediate cycle you happen to be plotting.

Once you have become accustomed to seeing the 3-4 month cycle in price charts, you will have a tremendous profit-making tool at your disposal. While you won't always be able to isolate the exact bottom of a given cycle, you will at least have in mind an approximate time frame of when to either buy or sell a given security. Cycle analysis, when combined with classical technical analysis and moving average analysis, provides a powerful combination that frequently makes all the difference in the world when it comes to interpreting a given chart pattern. For instance, there are times when analyzing price charts that a trader may have difficulty in trying to determine whether, say, a triangle pattern is a bullish continuation formation or a bearish distribution pattern. By counting the 3-4 month cycle on the chart, our trader can often accurately guess what the price will do upon reaching the "apex" of the triangle—whether the breakout will be to the upside or the downside based solely on the position (whether upward or downward) of the 3-4 month cycle. Note the examples, Figures 6-4 and 6-5, on pages 67 and 69.

Cycle analysis, when combined with classical technical analysis, provides a powerful one-two combination that frequently makes all the difference in the world when it comes to interpreting a given chart pattern.

Figure 6-4. Huffy (HUF)

Within this triangle pattern in Huffy's weekly chart, the first indication of a cycle bottom at the area labeled 1. The next bottom is at area 2, six months later, which indicates the 6-month cycle has bottomed. From here, prices rise three months into July—the precise mid-point of the 6-month cycle. The astute trader would know to sell out at this point since the ascending phase is complete. He would expect prices to break through the lower boundary of the triangle pattern, based on the fact that the 6-month cycle has three more months before bottoming and will act to carry prices lower. Sure enough, the next indication the 6-month cycle had bottomed came three months later in November (point 4).

From this example we can make another rule for identifying cycles within the context of chart patterns

A bear market is a period in which there is essentially a long decline in prices interrupted by important rallies, usually for a long time.

FIGURE 6-4: Two-year weekly chart with 30-week moving average.

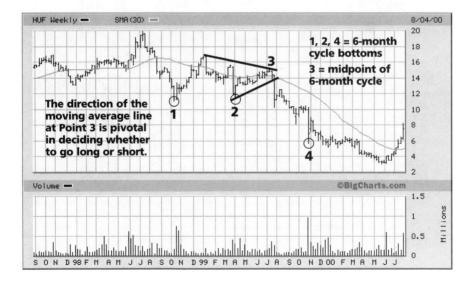

HUF Weekly ▬   SMA(30) ▬   8/04/00

1, 2, 4 = 6-month cycle bottoms
3 = midpoint of 6-month cycle

The direction of the moving average line at Point 3 is pivotal in deciding whether to go long or short.

Volume ▬   ©BigCharts.com

S O N D98F M A M J J A S O N D99F M A M J J A S O N D00 F M A M J J

The rule of thumb here is that the position of the moving average relative to the priceline within a chart pattern — especially as the pattern nears a breakout point — is pivotal to deciding whether to go long or go short the security you are trading.

as well as the moving average: whenever the price-line approaches the "apex," or tip, of a triangle pattern in a stock or commodity chart, watch carefully the position of the moving average at the apex. If the moving average has been rising or going sideways then turns up at the tip — even slightly — this is a very strong indication that the priceline will break out of the triangle pattern to the upside. Reverse this rule if the moving average turns down at the tip, especially if it has been falling before the triangle pattern formed. The rule of thumb here is that the position of the moving average relative to the priceline within a chart pattern — especially as the pattern nears a breakout point — is pivotal to deciding whether to go long or go short the security you are trading. Chart pattern analysis, moving average analysis, and cycle analysis, when used together, give the trader a powerful 1-2-3 combination for predicting price movements and beating the market.

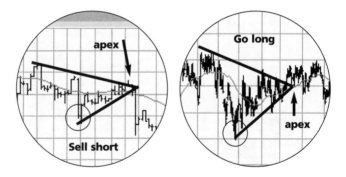

Note the apex in both examples and the direction the moving average is going at the tip of the apex. The downward sloping moving average in the example on the left indicates to sell short. The example on the right, strongly shows to go long as the moving average is pointing upward.

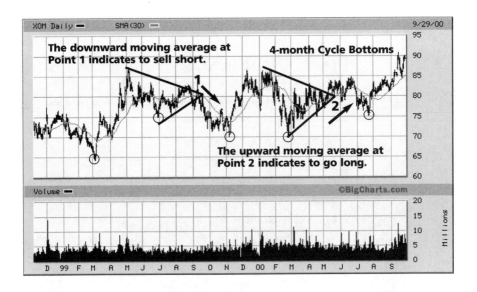

Figure 6-5. **ExxonMobil (XOM)**

Figure 6-5. ExxonMobil (XOM)

This triangle pattern in ExxonMobil's chart evinced a strong indication of a cycle bottom in March 2000, followed by another cycle bottom in July — four months later. The trader would have been justified in assuming that prices were due to break out of the triangle to the upside since a new 4-month cycle was underway, which proved to be the case. Note also how the moving average dipped in a bowl-shaped fashion before turning up at the apex of this triangle pattern in August. This was a strong confirmation of the bullish trend about to get underway.

Identifying 6-8 Month Cycle

Now that we have established the existence and reliability of the 3-4 month cycle, let us examine another time frame along the threeness and fourness cycle pattern. Just above the 3-4 month cycle series is the more significant 6-8 month cycle. This cycle occurs

FIGURE 6-5:
Daily chart with a 30-day moving average.

Bull market is the period in which prices are primarily rising, normally for an extended period.

with great regularity in most actively traded stocks and commodities and is a derivative of the 3-4 month cycle (being double this time frame). In cycle analysis, the Harmonic Principle applies to cycles of all sizes and time frames; this principle states that cycles within a given series of cycles can all be measured with reference to one another by a factor of half (e.g., the 3-4 month cycle is half the 6-8 month cycle, which in turn is half the 12-16 month cycle, etc.) The 6-8 month cycle tends to come down harder than its smaller component, the 3-4 month cycle. Notice the severity of the complete 6-8 month cycle in the chart example following.

Figure 6-6.   Citigroup (C)

FIGURE 6-6:
Two-year weekly
chart with a 30-
week moving
average.

Within this large wedge-shaped pattern in Citigroup, a strong seasonal tendency for a bottom in October can be seen. This equates to the one-year — or two 6-month cycles. The triangle first

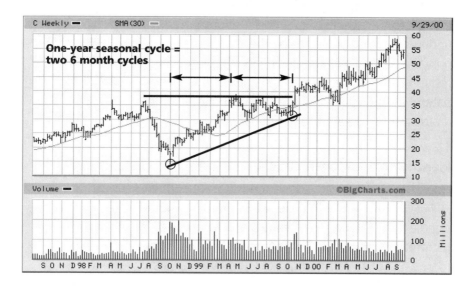

formed in October of 1998 (circled) area and completed its one-year cycle in October 1999 (circled).
Once the bottom was in, the trader could have
surmised that Citigroup's stock would break out of
the wedge pattern with the new cycle carrying its
price to higher levels.

Figure 6-7.
Dow Jones Industrial Average (DJIA)

As with the 3-4 month cycle, the 6-8 month cycle
should be interpreted with respect to its established
rhythm in a given security. For example, the chart for
the Dow Jones Industrial Average (DJIA) reflects a
well-established 3-month rhythm for its intermediate
cycle. We would be justified in assuming that its
larger 6-8 month cycle would come closer to filling
a 6-month rhythm, and indeed this is the case as
evidenced by the chart below.

**FIGURE 6-7:
One-year daily
chart using a
30-day moving
average.**

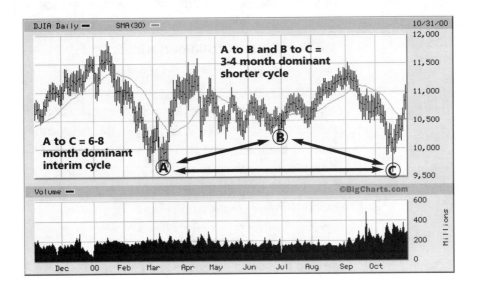

In analyzing cycles, the 6-8 month cycle should always be isolated first, then the 3-4 month cycle, then the 3-4 week cycle, which we discuss in the section below. Cycle analysis should always be performed from the largest cycle or family of cycles down to the smallest.

3-4 Week Cycles

Underneath the 3-4 month cycle can be found in most actively traded securities (stocks and commodities) a 3-4 week cycle. This equates to a 15-20 day cycle (since trading is done only on weekdays, each trading week being equal to 5 days). The 3-4 week cycle, while helpful and important, especially to short-term "swing" traders (i.e., traders who trade on short-term price movements), isn't as significant as the larger 3-4 month cycle. Nevertheless, its effects are felt across the broad spectrum of trading contracts, running the gamut of stocks and bonds, commodities and currencies.

3-4 Year Cycle (Kitchin or Business Cycle)

Yet another time frame along the threeness and fourness cycle rhythm is the 3-4 year cycle, known also as the Kitchin Cycle, or more commonly, as the Business Cycle. This particular cycle is the most significant of the three cycle families we have examined thus far as it exerts a profound influence on the broad stock market. It is less visible in the commodity markets than in stocks, but it does nevertheless show up even in that sector. The effects of the 3-4 year cycle were felt in the U.S. stock market; indeed, around the world, as equity and currency markets crumbled in late 1998 before rebounding toward the end of that year. The 3-4 year cycle contains its own "internal rhythm" so that an analyst can often predict when it will next begin its ascending phase by looking at the most recent cycle bottom. For example, the 3-4 year stock market cycle in the U.S. has shown a 3-year rhythm since 1987, when it bottomed in October of that year, producing a steep and violent decline in the equities market. Since the last bottom of this cycle in the fall of 1998, it is safe to assume that the mid-point, or crest, of the 3-year stock market cycle has been passed as of this writing, and that the next few months will see increasing downside pressure throughout the broad U.S. stock market.

Another interesting aspect to the 3-4 year Kitchin Cycle is that every Kitchin is typically composed of nine 3-4 month cycles, also known as "Wall Cycles" (after the man for whom they are named, P.Q. Wall). The number nine, of course, is yet another derivative of the number three in our Principle of Threeness and Fourness. This fact will allow for improved timing of the Kitchin Cycle since the trader knows that the closer to the bottom the of the nine-period (whether 9-week, 9-month, 18-week, 18-month, 36-week, 36-month, etc., or any other derivative of the number nine) cycle prices reach, the more strongly will its downward pressure be felt in the stocks and commodities you happen to be following. Combining Kitchin Cycle counting with Wall Cycle counting frequently leads to a degree of accuracy far higher than single cycle analysis would allow.

The 3-4 year cycle, known also as the Kitchin Cycle, or more commonly, as the Business Cycle is the most significant of the three cycle families we have examined thus far as it exerts a profound influence on the broad stock market.

Parts of a Cycle

An important thing to remember when analyzing cycles of all types and sizes is that a cycle can be divided into two equal parts, an ascending phase and a descending phase. Each cycle contains what is known as the "mid-point," which is the dividing line between the upward and the downward phase of the cycle. This is best illustrated by the geometric pattern known as the parabola shown below. Also shown is a closeup of a 3-month price cycle.

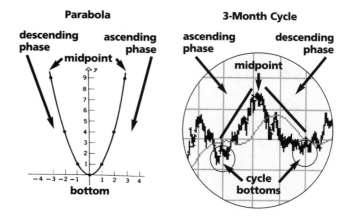

The rule of thumb when following cycles is to let the moving average line signal when prices are in the declining stage of the cycle, since moving averages are essentially distillations of the cycle and can tell you when to buy and sell much better than following the cycle without the use of moving averages.

Since every cycle has a mid-point, the cycle you happen to be examining can be theoretically divided into half from the perspective of time. For instance, if you are analyzing a price chart in search of the 3-4 month cycle, once you have isolated this cycle, you can divide each cycle into half, with the ascending phase of the cycle representing the first half and the descending phase representing the second half. In the case of a 3-month cycle, the theoretical mid-point of the cycle would be at 1½ months. This is not to say that every cycle peaks at exactly the theoretical mid-point; frequently prices can keep rising even after they have passed the mid-point of their respective cycles (especially if there is a larger cycle in the ascending phase underneath the cycle you happen to be analyzing). However, the theoretical mid-point of any given cycle should be considered a possible turning point for prices. Once prices have reached the two-thirds point of the cycle, it is highly doubtful they can mount a meaningful rally, but will almost certainly decline under the force of the descending phase of the cycle.

Figure 6-8.　General Motors (GM)

This daily chart of General Motors (GM) shows a 4-month cycle with mid-points indicated at points 1, 2, and 3 on the chart. Note how the midpoints at 2 and 3 were immediately followed by confirmed sell signals. However at point 1, the moving average starts to turn but goes sideways for a month and

FIGURE 6-8: Two-year daily chart with a 30-day moving average.

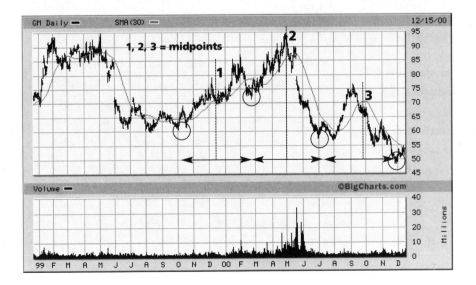

then turns upward with a confirmed sell signal in mid-February, almost immediately before the start of the next 4-month cycle.

Knowing where the mid-points of the cycles fall is important; however, just because a cycle passes its mid-point does not necessarily mean that prices will decline from that point forward. It sometimes happens that the priceline of the stock or commodity you are following will continue rising past the mid-point of the cycle for a while. This is due to the underlying strength of larger cycles — cycles which you may or may not be aware of — acting against the force of the smaller cycle you are following. The rule of thumb when following cycles is to let the moving average line signal when prices are in the declining stage of the cycle, since moving averages are essentially distillations of the cycle and can tell you when to buy and sell much better than following the cycle without the use of moving averages.

So to summarize, there exists a well-documented family of cycles that revolve around the three and four interval: the 3-4 week cycle, the 3-4 month cycle, and the 3-4 year cycle. Each cycle should be analyzed within the context of the others, and the trader should never attempt a cyclic analysis of any given chart without reference to the underlying and overlying cycles, lest his analysis become skewed. By determining the position of each of the three cycle families discussed here, a trader increases his odds of being able to profitably predict turns and movements in the markets.

Each cycle should be analyzed within the context of the others, and the trader should never attempt a cyclic analysis of any given chart without reference to the underlying and overlying cycles, lest his analysis become skewed. By determining the position of each of the three cycle families discussed in this chapter, a trader increases his odds of being able to profitably predict turns and movements in the markets.

There are, of course, other cycles besides the 3-4 rhythm cycles. But even most of these cycles are derivatives of the basic 3-4 interval cycle. Examples would include the 6-year cycle; the 8-12 year, or "Juglar" cycle; the 20-24 year cycle; and famous 60-year "Kondratieff Cycle," or "K-Wave." Each of these is important in its respective place, but for our purposes we will focus in this book on the smaller cycles, most notably the 3-4 month cycle (the most important of the intermediate-term cycles).

Our treatment of cycles paves the way for our discussion of using moving averages to identify support and resistance levels using the 3-4 interval cycle. In the following chapter we will examine the various applications of the 3-4 interval cycle with respect to moving averages, and how its use can greatly aid the trader in navigating the markets.

NOTES

1 *Technical Analysis of Stocks & Commodities*, November 1999, "Interview with Hamilton Lewis," pg. 82

2 P.Q. Wall publishes a monthly newsletter on cycles, P.Q. Wall Forecast, Inc., P.O. Box 15558, New Orleans, LA 70175, $198/12 issues.

CHAPTER 7

Using Moving Averages to Identify Support and Resistance Levels:
A Key Tool to Capture Tops and Bottoms

Besides being an extremely useful and profitable timing tool, moving averages can also be used as a gauge of support and resistance in a stock or commodity. Support and resistance, which represent demand and supply, respectively, are extremely important in any type of technical trading system, since an accurate forecast of any given security can only be performed with a knowledge of who has greater control over the market or security you are looking at — the buyers or the sellers. When once you've decided who holds greater control, your likelihood of trading success is much greater; thus, support and resistance analysis is crucial to any trading system.

Moving averages can also be used as a gauge of support and resistance — demand and supply — in a stock or commodity.

The well-known authorities on chart reading, Edwards & Magee, defined support as the "buying, actual or potential, sufficient in volume to halt a downtrend in prices for an appreciable period."[1] Resistance, of course, is the antithesis of this and consists of selling, actual or potential, in sufficient volume to keep prices from rising for a time. "Support and resistance, as thus defined, are nearly, but not quite, synonymous with demand and supply, respectively."[2]

Further expounding this concept, Edwards & Magee tell us:

"A support level is a price level at which sufficient demand for a stock appears to hold a downtrend temporarily at least, and possibly reverse it, i.e., start prices moving up again. A resistance zone by the same token, is a price level at which sufficient supply of a stock is forthcoming to stop, and possibly turn back, its uptrend. There is, theoretically, a certain amount of supply and a certain amount of demand at any given price level...But a support range represents a concentration of demand, and a resistance range represents a concentration of supply."[3]

Support is a level or area on the chart under the market where buying interest is sufficiently strong to overcome selling pressure and a decline is halted. A support level is usually identified beforehand by a previous reaction low.

In classical chart analysis, support and resistance are delineated using horizontal lines and channels. For instance, a stock chart of say, General Motors, might show a prolonged sideways price movement over a period of several weeks which can be highlighted by drawing two horizontal lines — one directly below the price congestion and one directly above. This shows the constant interplay between supply and demand, or the sellers and the buyers. Support and resistance can also be isolated when markets are moving along a trend line, either higher or lower. Think of the lower part of the price boundary as support (i.e., demand) and the upper part of the price range as resistance (i.e., supply). Successful traders think in terms of supply and demand whenever they look at a price chart since a chart is nothing more than a pictorial history of the interaction between buyers and sellers.

In a trending market, especially one in which prices travel within the confines of a clearly defined channel, the support and resistance lines will tend to keep prices within the boundaries. Thus, prices normally fluctuate within the channel, bouncing from support to resistance in an alternating "zig-zag" pattern.

But support and resistance are more than just upward trending or downward trending channel lines. Support and resistance may be encountered from a variety of chart patterns and other places of price congestion on the charts.

One rule of thumb for determining where a market or security will meet with either support or resistance on the charts is to find previous chart areas where consolidation has occurred. If, for example, a particular stock has stalled out in a net sideways or other congestion pattern at a certain level in the recent past before falling to a lower level, it is all but likely that the stock will encounter difficulty in penetrating that same level later on as it rallies and tries to overcome it. This, of course, does not necessarily mean that the former area of consolidation (in this case, resistance) will prove impenetrable; to the contrary, it will probably be overcome eventually. But not without considerable effort on behalf of the buyers. The greater the congestion, the greater the effort required to overcome that congestion, whether it is in the form of support or resistance.

Resistance is the opposite of support and represents a price level or area over the market where selling pressure exceeds buying pressure and a price advance is turned back. A resistance level is usually identified by a previous peak.

Thus, support and resistance serve as checks in the development of a trend (be it a rising or a falling trend) to keep the trend from moving too far, too fast and thus getting out of hand and eliciting violent reactions.

This leads us to the next related principle of support and resistance which Edwards & Magee elucidate for us:

The curving movement of the moving average(s) identify the areas of support and resistance.

". . . here is the interesting and the important fact which, curiously enough, many casual chart observers appear never to grasp: These critical price levels constantly switch their roles from support to resistance and from resistance to support. A former top, once it has been surpassed, becomes a bottom zone in a subsequent downtrend; and an old bottom, once it has been penetrated, becomes a top zone in a later advancing phase."[4]

Thus, if a certain security breaks through an overhead resistance level at, say $50, then the moment prices are above the $50 level, it automatically becomes a support. Conversely, if the $50 in our hypothetical security had been a support, checking prices from moving below it, and the $50 level is suddenly penetrated, then $50 automatically becomes resistance. This principle, which we will call the "principle of interchangeability," holds true for older levels of support and resistance as well, not just recent levels.

Moving Average Support and Resistance

Now that we have discussed the basics of support and resistance analysis we can proceed to the equally useful concept of moving average support and resistance. Under this concept, instead of drawing straight-edged diagonal or horizontal lines to delineate support and resistance, the trader merely lets the moving average(s) identify the areas of support and resistance. Using this method sometimes takes experimentation in order to find the optimal moving average time frame. For example, not all moving averages work for this technique—some moving averages might be too slow, others too fast. Therefore, work with different moving averages' time frames in order to determine the right length to use—a moving average that tends to capture most of the twists and turns, tops and bottoms along the chart.

The "proper" moving average length should be determined by how well it contains the priceline of the security you are following over a long period of time. In order to discover this you will need to perform a sufficient back-test of the chart you are following in order to decide the best moving average for trading purposes. Also, keep in mind you will want to adjust your averages according to the time frame of the chart you are following: for instance, for a daily chart you will want to use a short-term daily moving average; for a weekly chart use a weekly average; and for longer time frames use a longer-term average consistent with the chart itself.

Work with different moving average(s) time frames in order to determine the right length to use—ones that tend to capture most of the twists and turns, tops and bottoms along the chart. The optimal moving average time frame should be determined by how well it contains the priceline of the security you are following over a long period of time.

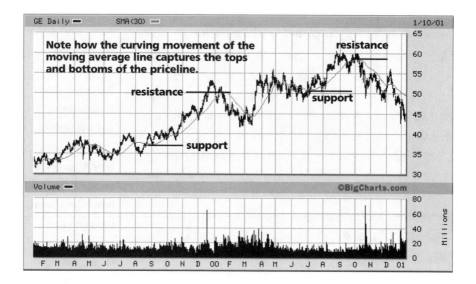

FIGURE 7-1:
General Electric
(GE) daily chart
with 30-day
moving average.

A prime example of how the moving average can act as a strong support is found in the daily chart for General Electric (GE). Notice the support the 30-day MA provided for GE's priceline between August and December of 1999. Each time GE threatened to sell off, the moving average acted to contain the slide, never once hesitating or drooping over but continuing to point higher throughout the last five months of 1999—a sign of technical strength.

Using moving averages as support and resistance identifiers in many ways is better than using traditional straight-edged lines, since prices in the real-world markets move along the timeline in a curving fashion, rather than straight up and down. Since moving averages follow this same curving movement, they are in many instances better suited to capture the tops and bottoms of the priceline (assuming, of course, you are using the proper moving average time frame).

Moving Average Time Frame Suggestions

Although each individual stock and commodity has its own unique series of cycles which govern its price movements, and will favor its own unique moving average time frame, a useful generalization can be stated:

- For daily charts of actively traded stocks, use a 30-day moving average and a 30-week moving average for weekly charts. This time frame seems to work best over a large number of stocks but is by no means equally suited to all stocks in all cases — this is merely a generalization based on years of observation.

- For commodities, use a shorter time frame for your moving averages; for instance, the 9-day and 18-day moving averages seem to work best for most agricultural commodities (for daily charts) and the 9-week and 18-week moving averages work well for weekly charts.

- For major stock indexes such as S&P 500, use a 50-day moving average for short-term support and resistance analysis and a 200-day moving average for the longer term. These two moving average series are widely followed by many financial institutions and large-scale traders, therefore they have great validity as support and resistance.

For the best results, do your own experimenting with various moving average lengths, using single averages and multiple averages as well.

For the best results, do your own experimenting with various moving average lengths, using single averages and multiple averages as well.

NOTES

1 Edwards & Magee, *Technical Analysis of Stock Trends*, Amacom, 1948, 1997, pg. 253

2 Ibid, pg. 254

3 Ibid, pg. 254

4 Ibid, pg. 254-255

Conclusion

A technically oriented trading system that uses moving averages of varying lengths to provide trading signals can be very profitable. Obviously, real-time experience and back-testing must be used in order to find the optimal moving average length, and the best results will come only with careful and continual practice.

It is the author's hope that you have gleaned from this book the essentials you will need to incorporate a profitable moving average system with your favored trading technique. It must be emphasized that moving averages will never take the place of old-fashioned "tape reading" and chart analysis; however, when used in tandem with these basic techniques and other market indicators, moving averages provide an ideal companion to any trading system. If nothing else, moving averages provide one of the best and most basic confirmation indicators available to the trader.

Moving averages can be used to trade virtually all markets and all time frames. The MA tends to work best in a trending market and, as we have explained,

Moving averages will never take the place of old-fashioned "tape reading" and chart analysis; however, when used in tandem with these basic techniques and other market indicators, moving averages provide an ideal companion to any trading system.

is best used in the intermediate time frame, with intermediate being defined as three-to-nine months. Our own personal favorite moving average time frame is the 30-period moving average (e.g., 30-hour, 30-day, 30-week, etc.), which tends to catch most of the important moves in any given market. Results using longer and shorter time frames are variable.

While the use of the moving average will never supplant a reliance on classical chart pattern analysis and tape reading, it can nevertheless greatly aid the trader in his analysis of the all-important market trend. Using the intermediate frame moving average for a trend-following approach is one of the applications best suited for a trading system that incorporates moving averages, and its potential as a profitable timing device is immense. Accordingly, we recommend it for this purpose.

Using a moving average or series of averages in a range-bound, or consolidation, market is not always suited for this technical approach. Moving averages work best when markets are in a well-defined ascending or descending phase. However, even in prolonged sideways markets, moving averages are ideal for use in conjunction with cycle analysis (as explained in Chapter 5) and provide excellent confirmation of important cycle bottoms.

A trading system using the double or triple crossover method is best suited for a trading market rather than a trending market. Multiple moving averages work best in a range-bound environment where a single moving average may not. The

No serious trader should use a trading system that does not incorporate some form of moving average tool. Even if the moving average is only used as a lagging, or confirming, indicator, it is a technical tool that provides many important signals to the active trader and has a variety of useful applications.

crossover method also works well as a turning point indicator. Using this technique, the trader can often pinpoint turning points in the price trends of stocks and commodities by noting when the shorter of the two moving averages crosses over and above (or underneath) the longer one (see Chapter 4 for an in-depth discussion of this technique plus chart examples).

In conclusion, we would emphasize that no serious trader should use a trading system that does not incorporate some form of moving average tool. Even if the moving average is only used as a lagging, or confirming, indicator, it is a technical tool that provides many important signals to the active trader and has a variety of useful applications. Always be wary of relying too heavily on moving averages alone. Again, they serve their best function when used in conjunction with basic technical analysis and should never be used in a vacuum. When used properly, and carefully tested, moving averages afford perhaps the best advantage a trader has of consistently trading the intermediate price cycle, of accurately forecasting turning points in the market, and of capturing the most dynamic portions of the intermediate and long-term trends.

When used properly, and carefully tested, moving averages afford perhaps the best advantage a trader has of consistently trading the intermediate price cycle, of accurately forecasting turning points in the market, and of capturing the most dynamic portions of the intermediate and long-term trends.

APPENDIX A

How to Calculate Moving Averages

Moving Averages

A moving average averages data in a specified period that "moves" in order to stay current with the present. A 200-day moving average, for example, moves so that it always represents the average of the last 200 days. In this discussion only averages of days will be referred to, but increments larger or smaller than days can be used when desired. There are two kinds of moving averages that we will discuss here — simple and exponentially weighted — and the variations of both kinds.

AUTHOR NOTE: **The following is a basic explanation of how various types of moving averages can be calculated and used.**

Simple Moving Average (SMA)

The simple moving average is calculated, as you can imagine, quite simply. Let's use an example of a 200-Day Moving Average (200-DMA). You add the data of whatever stock or futures contract you are following (such as, for example, the S&P 500) for the last 200 days, then divide the result by 200 (e.g., add each day's closing price for the past 200 trading sessions then divide the sum by 200). The result of this simple equation is then plotted as a point in the 200-day moving average. The next day, add the previous 200 days of closing prices for the

S&P 500 then divide by 200, then plot that number as the next point in the construction of your moving average). The average "moves" and changes each day as the oldest value is dropped out of the calculation and the new day's value added in.

In a simple moving average, every day's value is given equal weight, and the effect of large values dropping out of the calculation as the average moves can unduly affect the result, or skew the result in a way that may not be desirable.

Another disadvantage of the simple moving average is that data must be maintained for the entire period covered by the average. For the standard 200-DMA this can become quite cumbersome.

Exponentially Weighted Moving Average (EMA)

The exponentially weighted moving average (hereafter called the exponential average) has the advantage of giving the most weight to the most current value. Also it only requires that you maintain the value of the previous day's average rather than the data for the entire period being averaged, so it is very compact.

[Note: In this discussion the division symbol will be represented by the slash (/) and the multiplication symbol by the asterisk (*) in all formulas shown here so that they will resemble formulas used in spreadsheet software.]

EMA CALCULATION METHOD #1

To calculate an exponential average you must first calculate the EXPONENT, which is the element in

The only significant difference between the various types of moving averages is the weight assigned to the most recent price data. Simple moving averages apply equal weight to the prices.

the formula that determines the period of the moving average. This is done by dividing 2 by the number of days in the period being averaged. For example, the exponent for a 200-EMA is determined by dividing 2 by 200. The result is 0.01 (2/200=0.01).

After you have determined the exponent, you have to calculate a simple moving average for the specified period before you can begin the exponential weighting. The simple MA is only calculated once when setting up the exponential calculation.

Once you have computed the exponent and the simple MA, you are prepared to begin calculating the exponential average. The following is a key for the symbols in the formula.

PDA = Prior Day's Average (Begin with simple MA, thereafter PDA is an exponential value.)

Exp = Exponent

CDV = Current Day's Value (If you are averaging a stock price, CDV is today's price.)

EMA = Current Day's Exponential Moving Average

To calculate the exponential average, subtract PDA from CDV, multiply the remainder by Exp, and add the result to PDA (round to two places). Expressed as a formula:

$$((CDV-PDA)*Exp)+PDA = EMA$$

Using real numbers:

PDA = 52
Exp = 0.01 (200-DMA)
CDV = 49
$((49-52)*0.01)+52 = 51.97000$

The exponentially weighted moving average has the advantage of giving the most weight to the most current value. Also it only requires that you maintain the value of the previous day's average rather than the data for the entire period being averaged, so it is very compact.

EMA CALCULATION METHOD #2

This is the method commonly used in charting software for EMA calculations. The following is the formula for calculating the exponent for this method:

Exp = 2/Period + 1

For example, the exponent for a 200-EMA is determined by dividing 2 by 201. The result is 0.00995 (2/(200+1) = 0.00995). After you have determined the exponent, calculate a simple moving average for the specified period before beginning the exponential weighting. The simple MA is only calculated as a starting point in the calculation.

Once you have computed the exponent and the simple MA , you are prepared to begin calculating the exponential average. The following is a key for the symbols in the formula.

PDA = Prior Day's Average (Begin with simple MA, thereafter PDA is an exponential value.)

Exp = Exponent

CDV = Current Day's Value (If you are averaging a stock price, CDV is today's price.)

EMA = Current Day's Exponential Moving Average

The formula to calculate the exponential average with this method is:

(CDV * Exp) + (PDA * (1 - Exp)) = EMA

Using real numbers:

PDA = 52
Exp = 0.00995 (200 -EMA)
CDV = 49
(49 * 0.00995) + (52 * (1 - 0.00995)) = 51.97015

Triangular Moving Average

Triangular moving averages place the majority of the weight in the middle part of the price series. They are actually double-smoothed simple moving averages. The periods used in this type of moving average varies, depending on whether or not an odd or even number of time periods is used.

The following steps, excerpted from Steven B. Achelis' book, *Technical Analysis From A to Z*, explain how to calculate a 12-period (e.g., 12-hour, 12-day, 12-week, 12-month, etc.) triangular moving average.

1. Add 1 to the number of periods in the moving average (e.g., 12 plus 1 is 13).
2. Divide the sum from Step 1 by 2 (e.g., 13 divided by 2 is 6.5).
3. If the result of Step 2 contains a fractional portion, round the result up to the nearest integer (e.g., round 6.5 up to 7).
4. Using the value from Step 3 (i.e., 7), calculate a simple moving average of the closing prices (i.e., a 7-period simple moving average).
5. Again using the value from Step 3 (i.e., 7) calculate a simple moving average of the moving average calculated in Step 4 (i.e., a moving average of a moving average).

Triangular moving averages place the majority of the weight in the middle part of the price series. They are actually double-smoothed simple moving averages.

Variable Moving Average

A variable moving average is an exponential moving average that automatically adjusts the smoothing percentage based on the volatility of the data series. Writes Steven B. Achelis, in *Technical Analysis From A to Z*: "The more volatile the data, the more sensitive the smoothing constant used in the moving average calculation. Sensitivity is increased by giving more weight to the current data.

"Most moving average calculation methods are unable to compensate for trading range versus trending markets. During trading ranges (when prices move sideways in a narrow range) shorter-term moving averages tend to produce numerous false signals. In trending markets (when prices move up or down over an extended period) longer-term moving averages are slow to react to reversals in trend. By automatically adjusting the smoothing constant, a variable moving average is able to adjust its sensitivity, allowing it to perform better in both types of markets."

A variable moving average is an exponential moving average that automatically adjusts the smoothing percentage based on the volatility of the data series.

A variable moving average is calculated as follows:

$$(0.078 \ (VR) \ * \ Close) + (1 - 0.078 \ (VR) \ * \ Yesterday's \ Moving \ Avg.)$$

Where:

VR = The Volatility Ratio

The variable moving average was defined by Tushar Chande in an article that appeared in *Technical Analysis of Stocks and Commodities* in March 1992.

Weighted Moving Average

A weighted moving average is designed to put more weight on recent data and less weight on past data. A weighted moving average is calculated by multiplying each of the previous day's data by a weight, which in turn is based on the number of days in the moving average. Weighted moving averages are among the least recommended of moving averages since they tend to mask over important trading movements and can hide the effects of cycles.

How Moving Averages Are Used

The primary purpose of moving averages is to "smooth" data so that trends are more discernable. They are used to construct market indicators and to assist in interpretation of price charts.

Moving average crossovers can also be used as signals to buy and sell. This is normally done in two ways: (1) by watching for price to cross whatever moving average you may be using, or (2) running two moving averages of the same price or index, one faster than the other (for example, a 20-EMA and a 200-EMA), and buying or selling when the faster average crosses the slower.

The weakness of moving average buy and sell systems is that they will most likely become unprofitable when the stock or index begins moving sideways in a narrow trading range. Under these circumstances price never moves above or below the average far enough to become profitable.

Which Averaging Method to Use

Whether to use a simple of exponential average is a matter of preference. However, it has been the author's experience that the simple moving average tends to give superior buy and sell signals, is easier to calculate, and less liable to whipsaws than the more complex exponential moving average.

Glossary

accumulation

The first phase of a bull market. The period in which far-sighted investors begin to buy shares from discouraged or distressed sellers. Financial reports are usually at their worst and the public is completely disgusted with the stock market. Volume is only moderate but beginning to increase on the rallies.

accumulation/distribution

Momentum indicator that associates changes in price and volume. The indicator is based on the premise that the higher the volume that accompanies a price move, the more significant the price move.

advance/decline line

The advance/decline line is undoubtedly the most widely used measurement of market breadth. It is a cumulative total of the advancing/declining issues. When compared to the movement of the market index, the A/D line has proven to be an effective gauge of the stock market's strength. The A/D line has to confirm the market movements. The A/D line is calculated by subtracting the number of stocks which declined in price for the day from the number of stocks which advanced, and then adding this value to a cumulative total.

amplitude of cycle

Normally the amplitude of a cycle is a function of its duration; i.e. the longer the cycle the bigger the swing.

arithmetic scale

All units of measure on an arithmetic scale are plotted using the same vertical distance so that the difference in space between 2 and 4 is the same as that between 20 and 22. This scale is not particularly satisfactory for long-term price movements, since a rise from 2 to 4 represents a doubling of the price whereas a rise from 20 to 22 represents only a 10% increase.

bear market

Period in which there is essentially a long decline in prices interrupted by important rallies, usually for a long time. Bear markets generally consist of three phases. The first phase is distribution, the second is panic and the third is akin to a washout. Those investors who have held on through the first two phases finally give up during the third phase and liquidate.

bear spreading

The short sale of a future or option of a nearby month and the purchase of a distant contract. (One notable exception to this principle in the traditional commodity markets is the precious metals group. Bull and bear markets in gold, silver and platinum are led by the distant months.)

bear trap

Corrections in a bear market which can easily be confused with a reversal or a new bull market. If you are not careful, you can be washed out by a bear trap. Also, a signal which suggests that the rising trend of an index or stock has reversed, but which proves to be false.

bull market

A period in which prices are primarily rising, normally for an extended period. Usually, but not always, divisible into three phases. The first phase is accumulation. The second phase is one of a fairly steady advance with increasing volume. The third phase is marked by considerable activity as the public begins to recognize and attempt to profit from the rising market.

bull trap

A signal which suggests that the declining trend of an index or stock has reversed, but which proves to be false.

bull spreading

The purchase of a nearby futures/options contract and a short sale of a distant contract. In certain types of bull markets which are caused by a tightness in the supply/demand situation, the nearby contract months usually rise faster than the distant ones.

beta

Measurement of sensitivity to market movements. The trading cycle (four weeks) breaks down in two shorter alpha and beta cycles, with an average of two weeks each.

blow-offs

(Climatic top) A sharp advance accompanied by extraordinary volume; i.e. a much larger volume than the normal increase which signals the final "blow-off" of the trend. This is followed either by a reversal (or at least a period of stagnation, formation or consolidation) or by a correction.

bond market sector

The bond market (i.e. the long end) has three main sectors, which are classified according to issuer.

- US government
- Tax-exempt issuers (i.e. state and local governments)
- Corporate issuers

breadth (market)

Breadth relates to the number of issues participating in a move. A rally is considered suspect if the number of advancing issues diminishes as the rally develops. Conversely, if a decline is associated with increasingly fewer falling stocks, it is considered to be a bullish sign.

breakaway gap

The hole or gap in the chart which is created when a stock or commodity breaks out of an area pattern (areas on the bar chart where no trading has taken place). This gap usually occurs at the completion of an important price pattern and usually signals the beginning of a significant market move. Breakaway gaps usually occur on heavy volume. More often than not, breakaway gaps are not filled.

breakout

When a stock or commodity exits an area pattern.

buying pressure

Buying or selling pressure is measured by volume indicators. It measures the strength of the buying or selling.

call options

Options which give the buyer the right to buy the underlying contract or stock at a specific price within a certain period and which oblige the seller to sell the contract or stock for the premium received before the expiration of the designated time period.

cash index
Index expressed in money. This is in contrast to futures prices.

channel lines
The channel line, or the return line as it is sometimes called, is a line parallel to the basic trend line. It is the line in a bull market which is drawn parallel to the basic uptrend line which connects the lows.

coils
Another word for a symmetrical triangle. A symmetrical triangle is composed of a series of two or more rallies and reactions in which each succeeding peak is lower than its predecessor, and the bottom of each succeeding reaction is higher than its predecessor.

commodity options
Gives the holder the right, but not the obligation, to purchase (a call) or sell (a put) on an underlying futures contract at a specific price within a specific period of time.

composite market index
Composite average — A stock average comprised of the stocks which make up the Dow Jones Industrial Average (DJIA) and the Dow Jones Utility Average. Basically a market index composed of a selection of specific stocks.

confirmation
In a pattern, the confirmation is the point at which a stock or commodity exits a price pattern (whether a triangle, a rectangle,

a "flag," "wedge," etc.) in the expected direction by an amount of price and volume sufficient to meet minimum pattern requirements for a bona fide breakout. This is also true for oscillators (see definition below). To confirm a new high or a new low in a stock or commodity, an oscillator needs to reach a new high or low as well. Failure of the oscillator to confirm a new high or a new low is called divergence and would be considered an early indication of a potential reversal in direction.

congestion area

The sideways trading area from which area patterns evolve. Not all congestion periods produce a recognizable pattern however.

consolidation

Also called a continuation pattern, it is an area pattern which breaks out in the direction of the previous trend.

contrary opinion

A measure of sentiment is useful in assessing the majority view, from which a contrary opinion can be derived.

cycles

The prices of many commodities reflect seasonal cycles. Due to the agricultural nature of most commodities, these cycles are easily explained and understood. However, for securities the cyclical nature is more difficult to explain. Human nature is probably responsible.

decennial pattern

A pattern first cited by Edgar Lawrence Smith. It is a ten-year pattern, or cycle of stock price movements, which has essentially repeated itself over a 58-year period. The decennial pattern can be of greater value if it is used to identify where the strong and weak points usually occur and then to check whether other technical phenomena are consistent.

diffusion index
A diffusion index shows the percentage of indicators which are above their corresponding levels in a previous period (in this case, six months earlier). The indicators are the coincident economic indicators which tend to rise and fall coincidentally with the overall economy. These indicators thus provide a good approximation of the economy. For example: industrial production, consumer installment debt, the federal budget deficit and inflation.

distribution
The first phase of a bear market. During this first phase, far-sighted investors sense the fact that business earnings have reached an abnormal height and unload their holdings at an increasing pace (accumulation).

divergence
Divergence refers to a situation in which different delivery months, related markets or technical indicators fail to confirm one another. Divergence is a valuable concept in market analysis and one of the best early warning signals for impending trend reversals.

diversification
Limiting risk exposure by spreading the investments over different markets or instruments. The more negative the correlation between the markets, the more diversified the risk.

dominant cycle
Dominant cycles continuously affect futures prices and can be clearly identified. These cycles are the only ones of real value for

forecasting purposes. Most futures markets have at least five dominant cycles.

Long-term cycle	two or more years in length
Seasonal cycle	one year
Primary or intermediate cycle	9 to 26 weeks
Trading cycle	four weeks
Short-term cycle	several hours to several days

Dow theory

In 1897 Charles Dow developed two broad market averages. The industrial average included 12 blue-chip stocks, and the rail average was comprised of 20 railroad enterprises. The Dow theory resulted from a series of articles published by Charles Dow in the Wall Street Journal between 1900 and 1902. The Dow theory is the forerunner to most principles of modern technical analysis.

Basic tenets of the Dow theory:
- the averages discount everything;
- the market has three trends: primary, secondary and minor
- major trends have three phases;
- the averages must confirm each other;
- volume must confirm the trend (volume must expand in the direction of the major trend);
- a trend is assumed to be in effect until it gives definite signals that it has reversed.

downtrend

The trend is simply the direction of the market. A downtrend is a trend which is marked by descending peaks and troughs; in other words, lower subsequent highs and lower lows. An uptrend would be defined as a series of successively higher peaks and troughs (higher highs and higher lows).

Elliott Wave

Theory of market behavior devised by R.N. Elliott.

Basic tenets of the Elliott Wave principle:
- pattern, ratio and time, in that order of importance;
- pattern refers to the wave patterns or formations that comprise one of the most important elements of the theory;
- ratio analysis is useful for determining retracement points and price objectives by measuring the relationship between the different waves;
- and time is used to confirm wave patterns and ratios.

Basic concepts of the Elliott Wave principle:
- action is followed by reaction;
- there are five waves in the direction of the main trend, followed by three corrective waves;
- a 5-3 move completes a cycle. The 5-3 move then becomes two subdivisions of the next higher 5-3 wave; and
- the underlying 5-3 pattern remains constant although the time span of each may vary.

envelopes

An envelope is comprised of two moving averages. One moving average is shifted upward and the second moving average is shifted downward. Envelopes define the upper and lower boundaries of a stock's normal trading range.

exhaustion gap

The gap that appears near the end of a market move. Towards the end of an uptrend, prices leap forward with a final gasp. However, this forward leap quickly loses grounds and prices decrease within a couple of days or a week. When prices close under this last gap, it is usually a clear indication that the exhaustion gap has made its appearance. This is a classic example of when the filling of a gap in an uptrend has very bearish implications.

exponential smoothing

The exponentially smoothed moving average assigns a greater weight to the more recent price of the stock or commodity you are following. It is therefore a weighted moving average. Mathematically, a single exponential smoothing is calculated as follows:

- $X = (C-Xp)K+Xp$
- X is exponential smoothing for the current period.
- C is closing price for the current period.
- Xp is exponential smoothing for the previous period.
- K is smoothing constant, equal to 2/n + 1 for Compu Trac and 2/n for Back Trac.
- n is total number of periods in a simple moving average, which is roughly approximated by X.

failures

Normally, a failure is when a completed pattern is not confirmed by the direction of the following move. The failure (in the Elliott Wave) shows a situation in which, in a bull market for example, wave 5 breaks down into the required five waves, but fails to exceed the top of wave 3.

fan lines

Fan lines are trend lines used to identify reversals of price trend and are constructed as follows: Two extreme points are identified on the chart, usually an important top and bottom. A vertical line is then drawn from the second extreme to the beginning of the move. This vertical line is then divided by 38%, 50% and 62%, with lines drawn through each point from the beginning of the trend. These three lines should function as support and resistance points on subsequent reactions by measuring 38%, 50% and 62% Fibonacci retracements.

Fibonacci numbers

A number sequence rediscovered by the Italian mathematician Fibonacci. In his book, *Liber Abaci*, the Fibonacci sequence is first presented as a solution to a mathematical problem involving the reproduction rate of rabbits. The number sequence presented is 1, 1, 2, 3, 5, 8, 13, 21, 34, 55, and so on to infinity. In technical analysis, the Fibonacci numbers are used to predict or measure future moves in stocks or to predict retracement levels.

filter rules

The rule used in chart analysis for confirming a breakthrough or a breakout from a chart pattern. An example of a filter rule is the 3% penetration criterion. This price filter is used mainly for breaking off longer-term trend lines, but requires that the trend line be broken on a closing basis by at least 3%. Another example of the application of this rule, which was devised by Edwards & Magee in their seminal work, *Technical Analysis of the Stock Market*, is to buy a stock or commodity when the priceline of the chart breaks above the uppermost boundary of a pattern (say, for example, a "rectangle" consolidation pattern) by 3% or more. Conversely, the security in question would be sold if the priceline breaks below the lower boundary of the pattern by 3% or more. The 3% rule does not apply to some financial futures, such as the interest rate markets. Another example is a time filter, such as the two-day rule.

flags (continuation pattern)

A flag looks like a flag on the chart. That is, it looks like a flag if it appears in an uptrend. The picture is naturally upside down in a downtrend. It might be described as a small, compact parallelogram of price fluctuations, or a tilted rectangle which slopes back moderately against the prevailing trend.

flow of funds

Flow of funds analysis refers to the cash position of the different groups, such as mutual funds or large institutional accounts. The thinking here is that the larger the cash position, the more funds that are available for stock purchases. While these forms of analysis are generally considered to be of secondary importance, it often seems that stock market technicians place more reliance on them than on traditional market analysis.

Gann angles

Geometric angles drawn on price charts and used for analyzing trends, devised by market technician W.D. Gann. Gann divided price actions into eighths: 1/8, 2/8, ... 8/8. He also divided price actions into thirds: 1/3 and 2/3:

    1/8 = 12.5%
    2/8 = 25.0%
    1/3 = 33.0%
    3/8 = 37.5%
    4/8 = 50.0%
    5/8 = 62.5%
    2/3 = 67.0%
    6/8 = 75.0%
    7/8 = 87.5%
    8/8 = 100.0%

The 50% retracement is the most important to Gann. Gann believed that the other percentages were also present in market action, but with diminishing importance.

gaps

Gaps are simply areas on the bar chart where no trading has taken place. In an uptrend, for example, prices open above the highest price of the previous day, leaving a gap or open space on a chart which is not filled during the day. In a downtrend, the day's highest price is below the previous day's low. Upside gaps are signs of market strength, while downside gaps are usually signs of weakness.

group rotation

The overall market consists of many stock groups which are a reflection of the companies making up the various segments of the economy. The economy, defined by an aggregate measure such as Gross National Product (GNP), is either rising or falling at any given time. However, there are very few periods in which all segments are advancing or declining simultaneously. This is because the economy is not one homogeneous unit. Group rotation is the rotation within the different groups of stocks depending on at which stage the economic cycle is at the moment.

hedging

To obviate risk and avoid speculation. Another common technique used in hedging in the commodities market is to sell short a commodity futures contract (say, for instance, the December 2001 gold contract) while being simultaneously "long" (i.e., having purchased) the cash equivalent of the same future. For example, the trader has purchased physical gold bullion and wants to "hedge" his commitment by selling short a gold futures contract in the event the price of gold drops; this way he is afforded a certain amount of price protection for his investment. Options contracts can also be used for hedging purposes.

high-low indicator

The new high-low cumulative indicator is a long-term market momentum indicator. It is a cumulative total of the difference between the number of stocks reaching a new 52-week high and the number of stocks reaching a new 52-week low. This indicator provides a confirmation of the current trend. Most of the time the indicator will move in the same direction as the major market indices. However, when the indicator and market move in opposite directions (divergence), the market is likely to reverse.

insider
Any person who directly or indirectly owns more than 10% of any class of stock listed on a national exchange, or who is an officer or director of the company in question.

intermediate trend
An intermediate, or secondary, trend is the direction of the trend in a period from three weeks to as many months.

intra-day
A record of price data during the day, such as 15-minute bar charts. Intra-day charts and price data are of primary importance to "day traders" and other short-term traders. Intra-day charts record price movements of stocks and commodities, interest rates, currencies, etc., as they occur on a second-by-second, minute-by-minute, or hour-by-hour basis, rather than just the daily or weekly price movements. These intra-day charts are extremely important for the timing aspects of trading.

key reversal day
The term "key reversal day" is widely misunderstood. All one-day reversals are potential key reversal days, but only a few actually become key reversal days. Many of the one-day reversals represent nothing more than temporary pauses in the existing trend after which the trend resumes its course. The true key reversal day marks an important turning point, but it cannot be correctly identified as such until well after the fact; that is, not until after prices have moved significantly in the opposite direction from the prior trend.

Kondratieff cycle

The Kondratieff wave, a 54-year cycle, is named after a Russian economist. This is a long-term cycle identified in prices and economic activity. Since the cycle is extremely long term, it has repeated itself only three times in the stock market. The up-wave is characterized by rising prices, a growing economy and mildly bullish stock markets. The plateau is characterized by stable prices, peak economic capacity and strong bullish stock markets. The down-wave is characterized by falling prices, severe bear markets and often a major war.

limit move

A move limited by the uptick or downtick rule in commodity trading.

log scale

Prices plotted on ratio or log scales show equal distances for similar percentage moves. For example, a move from 10 to 20 (a 100% increase) would be the same distance on a log chart as a move from 20 to 40 or 40 to 80.

long-term cycle

A long-term cycle is basically two or more years in length.

major market trend

The major market trend is the primary direction of the market. The Dow theory classifies the major trend as being in effect for longer than a year. Futures traders would be inclined to shorten the major trend to anything longer than six months.

margin, commodities

The most important difference between stocks and commodity futures is the lower margin requirements on stock futures. All futures are traded at a margin, which is usually less than 10% of the value of the contract. The result of these low margin requirements is tremendous leverage. Relatively small price moves in either direction tend to be magnified according to their impact on overall trading results.

margin, stocks

This occurs when an investor pays part of the purchase price for a security and borrows the balance, usually from a broker; the margin is the difference between the market value of the stock and the loan which is made against it.

margin debt

Debt caused by margin requirements.

market averages

In stock market analysis, the starting point of all market analysis is always the broad market averages, such as the Dow Jones Average or the Standard & Poor's 500 Index. A market average is usually an index of the most important stocks in the market or a broad market index that covers 98-99% of the market as a whole.

member short sale ratio

The member short ratio (MSR) is a market sentiment indicator which measures the short selling activity of the members of the New York Stock Exchange. "Members" trade on the floor of the exchange, either on their own behalf or for their clients. Knowing what the "smart money" is doing is often a good indication of the near-term market direction. The MSR is the inverse of the Public Short Sale Ratio.

minor market trend

The minor, or near-term, trend usually lasts less than three weeks and represents shorter-term fluctuations in the intermediate trend.

momentum indicator

The momentum indicator measures the amount a security's price has changed over a given time span; in other words, the rate of change of a security's price over time. It displays the rate of change as a ratio.

most active stocks

The most active stocks are stocks which are traded the most over a certain period. Statistics on the most active stocks are published in the general press on both a daily and weekly basis. Usually the 20 most active stocks are recorded.

moving average

A moving average is the average of the closing prices of x periods added up and divided by x. The term "moving" is used because the calculation moves forward in time. Moving averages are used to help identify different kinds of trends (short-term, intermediate medium, etc.).

Also, a smoothing device with a time lag.

The moving average is one of the most versatile and widely used of all technical indicators. Because of the way it is constructed and the fact that it can be so easily quantified and tested, it is the basis for most mechanical trend-following systems in use today.

moving average crossovers

One moving average method used by technicians. A buy signal is produced when the shorter average crosses above the longer-term moving average. Two popular combinations are the 5- and 20-day averages and the 10- and 40-day averages.

neckline

Support or resistance level in a head and shoulders chart pattern. The "neckline" is a horizontal line drawn on the chart which connects the lows or highs of the "shoulders" (i.e., the extreme left-hand and right-hand sides of the pattern) depending on whether the pattern is in its top phase or bottom phase.

nominality

The principle of nominality is based on the premise that, despite the differences which exist in the various markets and allowing for some variation in implementing cyclical principles, there seems to be a set of harmonically related cycles which affect all markets. A nominal model of cycle lengths can be used as a starting point for any market.

odd-lot ratios

There are a few odd-lot ratios:
- Odd-lot balance index (OLBI)
- Odd-lot short ratio
- Odd-lot purchases/sales

The OLBI is a market sentiment indicator that shows the ratio of odd-lot sales to purchases (an "odd-lot" is a stock transaction of less than 100 shares). The assumption is that "odd-lotters", the market's smallest traders, do not know what they are doing. When the odd-lot balance index is high, odd-lotters are selling more than they are buying and are therefore bearish on the market. To trade contrarily to the odd-lotters, you should buy when they are selling.

on-balance volume

On-balance volume (OBV) is a momentum indicator which relates volume to price. The OBV is a running total of volume. It shows whether volume is flowing into or out of a security. When the security closes higher than the previous close, all of the day's volume is considered up-volume. When the security closes lower than the previous close, all of the day's volume is considered down-volume. The basic assumption in OBV analysis is that OBV changes precede price changes. The theory is that smart money can be seen as flowing into a security by a rising OBV. When the public then moves into a security, both the security and the OBV will surge ahead.

open interest

Open interest is the number of open contracts of a given futures or options contract. An open contract can be a long or short open contract which has not been exercised, or has been closed out or allowed to expire. Open interest is really more a data field than an indicator.

oscillators

Any of various technical indicators based on price fluctuations. The methods used in creating such an indicator are too complex to be explained here and are usually performed with the aid of a computer (see any of the several books on oscillator construction and technique available from *www.Traderslibrary.com*). The oscillator is extremely useful in non-trending markets where prices fluctuate in a horizontal price band, or trading range, creating a market situation in which most trend-following systems simply do not work that well. The three most important uses for the oscillator are:

- The oscillator is most useful when its value reaches an extreme reading near the upper or lower end of its boundaries. The market is said to be overbought when it is near the upper extreme and oversold when it is near the lower extreme. This warns that the price trend is overextended and vulnerable;
- A divergence between the oscillator and the price action when the oscillator is in an extreme position is usually an important warning signal; and
- Crossing the zero line can give important trading signals in the direction of the price trend.

overbought level

An opinion on the price level. It may refer to a specific indicator or to the market as a whole after a period of vigorous buying, after which it may be argued that prices are overextended for the time being, and are in need of a period of downward or horizontal adjustment.

oversold level

An opinion on the price level. A price move that has overextended itself on the downside.

over owned stocks

A stock is over owned when fashion-conscious investors are all interested in buying a certain stock.

Point & Figure

Method of charting prices. A new plot on a P&F chart is made only when the price changes by a given amount. P&F charts are only concerned with measuring price. P&F charts are constructed using combinations of X's and 0's known as "boxes." The X shows that prices are moving up, the 0 that they are moving down. The size of the box and the amount of the reversal are important.

primary trend

This is the most important long-term trend. A primary trend usually consists of five intermediate trends. Three of the trends form part of the prevailing trend while the remaining two run counter to that trend.

public/specialist short sale ratio

It measures the round-lot short selling by the public against the New York Stock Exchange specialists on the floor of the exchange. It pits the smart money against one of the least informed categories of market participants.

rally
A brisk rise following a decline or consolidation of the general price level of the market.

reaction
A temporary price weakness following an upswing.

relative strength (RS)
An RS line or index is calculated by dividing one price by another. Usually the divisor is a measure of "the market," such as the DJIA or the Commodity Research Bureau (CRB) Index. A rising line indicates that the index or stock is performing better than "the market" and vice versa. Trends in the RS can be monitored by moving average crossovers, trend line breaks, etc. in the same way as any other indicator.

resistance
Resistance is the opposite of support and represents a price level or area over the market where selling pressure overcomes buying pressure and a price advance is turned back. A resistance level is usually identified by a previous peak.

retracement
Retracements are basically countertrend moves. After a particular market move, prices retrace a portion of the previous trend before resuming the move in the original direction. These countertrend moves tend to fall into certain predictable percentage parameters. The best known application of this phenomenon is the 50% retracement. For example: a market is trending higher and travels from the 100 level to the 200 level. The subsequent reaction very often retraces about half of the prior move.

seasonal cycle
Seasonal cycles are cycles caused by the seasonal changes in the supply-demand relationship (caused by factors which occur at about the same time every year).

secondary trend
Secondary trends are corrections in the primary trend and usually consist of shorter waves that would be identified as near-term dips and rallies.

sentiment indicator
Indicators, which measure the market sentiment, such as:
- Specialist Public Ratio
- Short Interest Ratio
- Insider Trading
- Advisory Services

short interest
The short interest is a figure published around the end of the month citing the number of shares that have been sold short on the NYSE.

speed resistance lines
Technique which combines the trend line with percentage retracements. The speed resistance lines measure the rate of a trend's ascent or descent (in other words, its speed).

stock index futures
Futures contract on indices.

support area
Support is a level or area on the chart under the market where buying interest is sufficiently strong to overcome selling pressure.

As a result, a decline is halted and prices turn back up again. A support level is usually identified beforehand by a previous reaction low.

trend line

A trend line is a straight line drawn up to the right, which connects important points in a chart. An up trend line is a line which connects the successive reaction lows, a down trend line connects the successive rally peaks.

upside/downside volume

Measurements of upside/downside volume try to separate the trading volume on a stock market exchange (such as the NASDAQ or the New York Stock Exchange) into advancing and declining stocks. By using this technique, which measures the ratio of advancing volume minus declining volume, or advancing volume divided by declining volume, it can be subtly determined whether accumulation or distribution is taking place in the overall market.

volume

Volume represents the total amount of trading activity in that market or stock over a given period.

whipsaws

Misleading moves or breakouts.

Trading Resource Guide
Tools for Success in Trading

Suggested Reading List

Trader's Guide to Technical Analysis

by C. Colburn Hardy

Achieving high-impact results can be made easier by implementing the most effective technical analysis tools throughout your trading day. In this easy-to-read classic, you will learn when to buy and sell stocks with the help of technical analysis — written for the average investor.

You will also learn to recognize trends and pinpoint entry points, and how to improve trading results by combining technical and fundamental tools and techniques.

$25.00, Item #2388.

Trend Forecasting With Technical Analysis
Unleashing the Hidden Power of Intermarket Analysis to Beat the Market

by Louis B. Mendelsohn

Market methods from the last century won't work in this one and Louis B. Mendelsohn's breakthrough book takes technical analysis to a new level. Mendelsohn presents a comprehensive approach combining technical and intermarket analysis into one powerful framework for accurately forecasting trends.

$19.95, Item #11836.

To order any book listed — and get a 20% discount — call 1-800-272-2855 ext. T140

New Thinking in Technical Analysis
Trading Models From the Masters
by Rick Bensignor

When pinpointing the best time to buy or take profits, technical analysis is the only true predictor of price behavior. Now discover the proven methods of the top traders adapted for today's markets. Learn how to use each model, when to use it, and when not to.

$55.00, Item #11706

Strategies for Profiting With Japanese Candlestick Charts (Video)
by Steve Nison

What are Japanese Candlesticks and why—and how—should traders use them? This brand new video workshop will help you understand and master this powerful tool with high-impact results. Steve Nison is the premiere expert on Candlesticks in the world and now you can benefit from his expertise in the comfort of your own home. Discover: The Most Important Candle Patterns, Using the Power of Candles for Online Trading, Combining Western Technical Indicators With Candlestick Charts for Increased Profits—and so much more!

Retail $695. Your price $395. Item #11727

Encyclopedia of Chart Patterns
by Thomas N. Bulkowski

Brand new, comprehensive guide covers chart formations, identifies chart patterns, explains market behavior, and provides up-to-date performance statistics on which patterns presage different market events. This thorough new work from a *Technical Analysis of Stocks and Commodities* magazine writer shows what failed patterns look like and why they failed, offers winning trading tactics, and highlights indicators that help identify and chart important trends.

$79.95, Item #10781

Reminiscences of a Stock Operator

by Edwin LeFevre

Generations of investors have benefited from this 1923 master-piece. Jack Schwager's new introduction explains why this account of Jesse Livermore, one of the greatest speculators ever, continues to be the most widely read book by the trading community.

19.95, Item #2116

Trader's Tax Solution
Money Saving Strategies for the Serious Investor

by Ted Tesser

Whether you're a professional trader, an occasional trader, or novice starting out, you need to guard your hard-earned profits from the tax man. Let tax pro Ted Tesser show how to set up your trading business from an accounting standpoint so that you can slash your tax liability to the bone. Just one small tip can cover the cost of the book — and save you thousands.

$59.95, Item #11074

New Market Wizards

by Jack Schwager

Meet a new generation of market killers. These winning traders make millions — often in hours — and consistently out-perform peers. Trading across a spectrum of financial markets, they use different methods but share remarkable successes. How do they do it? How can you do it? Learn their successful trading tactics.

$39.95, Item #2106

Internet Sites

Traders' Library Bookstore . . . . **www.traderslibrary.com**
The #1 source for trading and investment books, videos and related products.

Clif Droke Web Site . . . . **www.tapetellsall.com**
This site contains a special section dedicated to forecasting markets using Elliott Wave Theory. The site also provides market commentary and forecasts based on principles from the author's books including *Elliott Wave Simplified* and *Technical Analysis Simplified*, as well as information about the "lost art" of tape reading — the interpretation of price-to-volume configurations in stocks and commodities.

BigCharts.com . . . . **www.bigcharts.com**
A comprehensive and easy-to-use investment research web site providing access to research tools including interactive charts, quotes, industry analysis, market news and commentary. The site also features intuitive navigation and compelling graphics.

Equis . . . . **www.equis.com**
Creators of MetaStock, the popular technical analysis software, this site offers a full range of powerful technical analysis tools for more profitable investing.

Bridge Financial . . . . **www.crbindex.com**
A comprehensive source of products and services for futures and options traders. This "onestop" site offers current quotes, online data, books, software products, news, and information from one of the world's leading financial information sources.

Martin Pring IIER . . . . **www.pring.com**
This site is dedicated to teaching the art of technical analysis and charting.

Wall Street Directory . . . . **www.wsdinc.com**
The best directory of financial sites on the web. A comprehensive site to help you find the answers to your financial questions and point you in the right direction.

Dorsey Wright . . . . **www.dorseywright.com**
The top source for information on Point & Figure analysis and comprehensive Point & Figure charts.

Equity Analytics. . . . . **www.eanalytics.com**
An excellent educational resource with extensive glossaries for technical analysis and many other topics.

Future Source . . . . **www.futuresource.com**
A comprehensive source of information for futures and other traders providing futures quotes, settlement prices, charts, FWN news, chat rooms and other useful tools for traders of all levels.

Track Data. . . . . **www.tdc.com**
A supplier of electronically delivered financial data since 1981 with several services specifically designed to assist day traders. Timely market data, financial databases, historical information, data manipulation tools and analytical services are available.

Bloomberg . . . . **www.bloomberg.com**
This major financial web site has it all—news, quotes, hot market information, lifestyle updates, investing tools, resources, and more. Turn to the industry leader for all your financial needs.

The Parabolic Report

Features a unique "parabolic" approach to analyzing price graphs . . .

Frequency: Biweekly (26 issues/yr.)

Subscription Price: $49.95

Editor: Clif Droke

Markets Covered: Stocks, stock indexes, interest rates, commodities, currencies

*T*he Parabolic Report provides in-depth technical analysis of all major U.S. and world stock markets and currencies, U.S. interest rates, and select commodities (precious metals, meats, and grains). The newsletter is unique in its "parabolic" approach to analyzing price graphs — a revolutionary new and scientific form of chart analysis with far greater accuracy and forecasting potential than classical technical analysis. The parabolic analysis contained in each issue of the newsletter isolates the dominant cycles which control the price movements of all actively traded stocks and commodities, providing the trader with a far greater margin for profit than afforded by other forms of market analysis. *The Parabolic Report* is published every other week at the unbeatable price of $49.95/yr.

For a FREE sample issue e-mail or write:
cdroke9819@aol.com

Clif Droke • 816 Easely Street, #411 • Silver Springs, MD 20901

About the Author

C LIF DROKE is a popular technical analyst, newsletter editor and author. He is the editor of *The Parabolic Report, a* biweekly newsletter, and the *Leading Indicators* newsletter, a weekly publication covering U.S. equities markets and socio-cultural trends from a technical perspective. He is also the editor of other newsletters, including *Clif Droke's Internet Stock Outlook* and the *Gold Strategies Review*. For these investment and trading publications, he analyzes several major sectors of the U.S. and global equities markets using the principles he outlines in *Moving Averages Simplified*.

Moving Averages Simplified is the third book he has authored in the Traders' Library Simplified Series. In the first book, *Technical Analysis Simplified,* Droke distills the essential elements of technical analysis into one powerful volume—covering all the basics: The Dow Theory, pattern recognition, volume, breadth, reliability of chart patterns, support and resistance, trendlines and channels, and one-day reversals. Martin Pring says *Technical Analysis Simplified* is "a great primer covering all the technical analysis basics every active investor needs to know."

In his second book, *Elliott Wave Simplified,* Droke takes the mystery out of using this effective technique—without being deluged with details. *Stocks & Commodities Magazine* says: "Hits the mark where most others on the subject fail . . . reveals a few new tricks even the advanced student will find useful." Included are the basics of technical analysis and R.N. Elliott's simple and proven theory, plus common pitfalls made when using Elliott Wave, as well as how the theory relates to trading volume, contrary opinion, channel analysis, the fan principle, filtered waves and more.

All three books are available at
www.traderslibrary.com

Free 2-Week Trial Offer for U.S. Residents From Investor's Business Daily:

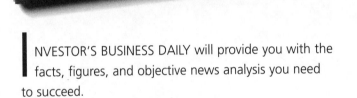

NVESTOR'S BUSINESS DAILY will provide you with the facts, figures, and objective news analysis you need to succeed.

Investor's Business Daily is formatted for a quick and concise read to help you make informed and profitable decisions.

To take advantage of this free 2-week trial offer, e-mail us at customerservice@traderslibrary.com or visit our web site at www.traderslibrary.com where you find other free offers as well.

You can also reach us by calling 1-800-272-2855 or fax us at 410-964-0027.

Notes

Notes

Notes

MOVING AVERAGES SIMPLIFIED

Notes

Notes

Notes

Notes

MOVING AVERAGES SIMPLIFIED

Notes